Income From
Your Home Computer

Income From
Your Home Computer

Edward J. Lias

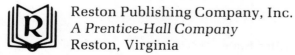

Reston Publishing Company, Inc.
A Prentice-Hall Company
Reston, Virginia

Library of Congress Cataloging in Publication Data

```
Lias, Edward J.
    Income from your home computer.

    Includes index.
    1. Home-based businesses.  2. Microcomputers.
I. Title.
HD62.7.L5  1983        001.64'04'068        82-21470
ISBN 0-8359-3047-5
ISBN 0-8359-3046-7 (pbk.)
```

Apple is a registered trademark of Apple Computer Company, Inc.

Atari is a registered trademark of Atari, Inc. (a Warner Communications Company).

Bell & Howell is a registered trademark of Bell & Howell.

CBM is a registered trademark of Commodore Business Machines, Inc.

CompuVend is a registered trademark of CompuVend Computer Services, Inc.

IBM is a registered trademark of International Business Machines Corporation.

Jinsam is a trademark of Jini Micro-Systems, Inc.

Osborne is a registered trademark of Osborne Computer Corporation.

PET is a registered trademark of Commodore Business Machines, Inc.

Rainbow is a registered trademark of Digital Equipment Corporation.

The Source is a service mark of Source Telecomputing Corporation, a subsidiary of The Reader's Digest Association, Inc.

TI Home Computer os a trademark of Texas Instruments.

Timex-Sinclair is a trademark of Sinclair technology under a license from Sinclair Research Ltd.

TRS-80 is a registered trademark of the Radio Shack division of Tandy Corporation.

VIC 20 is a registered trademark of Commodore Business Machines, Inc.

10 9 8 7 6 5 4 3 2 1

Printed in the United States of America

Contents

6 SETTING UP MICROCOMPUTER APPLICATIONS FOR PROFIT 67

7 CONNECTING MICROS TO THE WORLD (FOR HARDWARE BUFFS) 79

8 TURNING YOUR WORD PROCESSOR INTO GOLD 87

9 STARTING A MICROCOMPUTER DEALERSHIP: ACTION AND MONEY 93

Introduction

This is the new age of home and cottage industries, and you can be part of it. Never before in history have there been so many opportunities for people to work at home producing goods and services that benefit thousands of other people throughout the nation. The desktop microcomputer makes it possible to provide dozens of services from which income can be realized. And almost any one can do it—including you!

More than two million desktop computers have been purchased in the United States since 1977 when Commodore and Radio Shack announced their versions of the "under $1,000" computer. That's a lot of computers, but would you believe that about three-fourths of them aren't used? Many are gathering dust or have been abandoned in closets after an initial surge of interest. These cobweb-covered microcomputers are capable of producing income—even if they are somewhat old or obsolete.

If you presently own one of these computers—or are about to

buy one—you'll find plenty of fantastic income opportunities described in this book. Read about them . . . think about them . . . follow through on one or many of them.

Even the microcomputer companies have difficulty keeping their employees. When you work inside the industry (as I did) you become more conscious of the fabulous moneymaking opportunities available to microcomputer owners, and you get to meet people who, in just a few years, achieved financial security by capitalizing on the ideas in this book.

You'll probably think of angles or opportunities beyond the thirty options presented here. Hopefully, this book will stimulate your creative mind to invent new ways to earn money from your microcomputer.

Readers of this book may vary from the naive to the super-sophisticated. Your breadth of experience—or lack of it—should not prevent you from reaping the income benefits. Which class do you fit into?

Over 500,000 VIC-20 microcomputers were sold in 1982 after Commodore introduced it. It is sold in department stores for under $200.

- Computer illiterate, having never touched or used a microcomputer.
- Owner of a TV game computer.
- Owner of a desktop microcomputer, but do not know how to use it.
- Can run simple programs that others have written, but cannot write programs.
- Can write simple programs in BASIC.
- Can operate one or two computer packages such as word processing or VisiCalc®[1].
- Know how to write complex BASIC programs with matrix handling and complex graphics.
- Know how to write programs in several languages, such as Pascal, APL, FORTRAN, etc.
- Know how to connect microcomputers to distant databanks to obtain information.
- Know how to connect microcomputers to distant mainframe computers for complex distributed processing.
- Know how to design large systems of programs for others to use.
- Know how to design circuits that attach to microcomputers, enabling them to control windows, lights, engines, etc.
- Can design computer hardware and digital circuits.

All the groups mentioned here are eligible to earn income from their desktop microcomputers. People in the first two categories may have to invest in more substantial equipment, but they are not excluded from moneymaking opportunities. This book tells why and how.

---

[1]VisiCalc® is a registered trademark of Personal Software, Inc., VisiCorp.

Income From Your Home Computer

Have Computer, Will Tutor

MONEY OPTION	**1**	Tutor about the Hookup and Operation of the Hardware
MONEY OPTION	**2**	Tutor in the Use of Computer Applications
MONEY OPTION	**3**	Tutor in the Various Microcomputer Languages
MONEY OPTION	**4**	Consult on Resources and Options

Private tutoring is a time-honored profession, and there are surprising reasons why microcomputers spawn a new breed of tutors and learners. Even if you never taught anyone anything (which, of course, you have), and although you may not know the BASIC language and have never learned to use word processing, this chapter will present potential income opportunities that do not cost anything except time and ambition.

There are many levels of learners when it comes to microcomputers. Some people want to learn about microcomputers for pleasure. Some people have hobbies they hope to support with microcomputers. Some parents want their children to receive private tutoring. Some children want their parents to receive private tutoring. Some small businesses want their clerks or bookkeepers to receive instruction about how to use micros. Which level would your skills match?

If schoolteachers come to you for tutoring about micros, they may often *prefer* private lessons rather than open workshop instruction. A traditional workshop arena with its twelve or fifteen micros becomes a showplace where slowness to learn may be remembered by peers long after the workshop is over. Schoolteachers are sometimes willing to pay extra for private tutoring.

Therefore, your home or den can be made into a private classroom where people come one at a time by appointment to practice using your microcomputer or to receive your counsel.

Several objections to this idea might be raised:

- "I don't know enough about micros to teach anyone."
- "No one would pay for what I know."

- "I don't want strangers learning where I live and the layout of my house."
- "I've already told my friends everything I know."

The third objection—strangers in the house—is a real problem. Perhaps you could arrange to prescreen your students at a local meeting place where you could give them some printed information, and then set an appointment at your house (or theirs) if they pass your screening test. Private tutoring implies a trusting relationship on *both* sides, of course. For that reason, you too should dress professionally and converse in a credible, trustworthy manner.

The fourth objection—my friends already took my course—overlooks the promotional opportunities existing for posting flyers about your services at local schools, computer stores, grocery store bulletin boards, and churches. Your nonpaying friends are not your only source of students. Before posting your flyer, be sure to ask the store owner or other authority for permission to display it.

Dozens of microcomputers are sold to new buyers each week in most towns, and waves of questions perpetually surface. If you are available to these people with timely answers, many who have spent $300 to $5,000 for a microcomputer may be pleased to pay $15 per hour for your instruction or assistance.

Four popular subjects dominate requests for tutoring. Tutors who lack knowledge in the last three areas can still earn income if they know something about the first one. The four subjects in which people desire tutoring are:

1. *Operations*—"How do I hook it up, turn it on, load cassettes or disks, etc.?"
2. *Applications*—"How can I learn to do word processing?"
3. *Languages*—"How can I write programs in BASIC?"
4. *Resources*—"What should I buy to make it play music or talk?"

Tutor About the Hookup and
Operation of the Hardware[1]

Although instruction manuals come in the microcomputer boxes, they are sometimes written like lawn mower assembly charts by engineers who do not explain in layman's terms the basic cabling and operating procedures that must be performed.

Just because you were able to get your computer hooked together and running, don't assume that everyone else is able to cable theirs into a working system. Some people just don't want to be bothered thinking about the wiring and cabling, and for that reason, local store managers might be willing to distribute your business cards along with the machines they sell. Your cards advertising set-up assistance could signal a welcomed service — both to the dealer and to the buyer.

Some people keep calling the store dealer far beyond his or her ability to respond. The dealer may have earned a limited profit on the microcomputer sale, from which the shipping bills, store rent, and commissions must be paid.

Dealers may wish to provide auxiliary services to their customers, but since they have a limited profit margin, their primary interest is in selling computers. Therefore, your tutorial services may be useful to them when customers keep calling their stores with questions.

Micros that attach to television sets sometimes have cable diagrams like city maps. Not everyone is willing to read the directions and, on call, you could help them connect the components together, adjust the television to the required channel, set the fine tuning so all of the colors are vivid, and raise the volume so the sound comes through.

The skills of plugging in cartridges, tape cassettes, disk drives, printers, modems, TV sets, loud speakers, joy sticks, or light pens are simple enough after several tries, but the fear of breaking a new, expensive computer can stall the newcomer for days.

When you are teaching, be sure that *the student* is seated at

---

[1]*Hardware* refers to computer machinery; *software* refers to the programs used to operate this equipment.

the micro and is doing the things you suggest. Novice teachers will be tempted to sit themselves down in front of the keyboard, slide the cables into place, hit a few keys, and say, "See, there's nothing to it." In such cases, the student will probably retain nothing and may not be able to locate the on-off switch when the teacher leaves.

Instead, with the learner seated at the micro, you should by pointing and describing direct the act of assembly, cabling, turning on, loading programs, and so on. Get *the learner* to do this under your direction.

K. Jenkin bought a microcomputer that attached to the TV set. It had a tape recorder with it for loading programs from cassette tape. The instructions didn't tell him to raise the volume on the TV set, so many months passed before he learned that sound accompanied the programs. Also, the programs often failed to

Photo courtesy of Radio Shack, a division of Tandy Corporation.

load properly, and the instructions did not state that the tape recorder should be placed far away from the TV set's radiation for more reliable loading.

Many new users have no idea what table arrangement is desirable; what shelving is necessary for manuals, disks, software, and printouts; nor how to care for disks and tapes. Therefore, the aggressive teacher will supply handouts showing such things as several preferred desk and table arrangements, an instruction sheet describing how to handle disks and tapes, a list of commonly used BASIC verbs, a glossary of terms, and clear directions for backing up tapes or disks.

If you wish to offer further tutoring in application systems, languages, or other follow-up consulting, be sure to present cheerful and useful guidance at the first session. You will more likely be asked to give a second and third lesson if you present the right combination of friendliness and professional distance at the first session. One or two pages describing your other services should be printed for promotion.

Charges for your tutoring will vary depending on whether the student travels to your home or you travel to his or her home. The charges might vary from $15 to $20 per hour depending on your skills, the image you present, and the demand in your area.

Computer store owners sometimes need help when they deliver ten or twenty microcomputer systems to schools or colleges. The task of opening the boxes, setting up the gear, cabling, and testing can take several hours.

Consider the value of making yourself available to the store dealer without charge on such occasions. Make yourself useful. The dealer will be more motivated to pass tutorial business to you, and you will have an opportunity to pass your business cards to teachers, school superintendents, and even the students.

If you are good at what you do, the store owner may pay you to offer instruction in a weekly seminar, or the store may include your personalized services for new customers as part of the deal when they buy a system.

Don't forget that department stores sell hundreds of microcomputers each week that cost $150 to $600. Even fewer services accompany these sales because the transaction is geared to mass distribution. Don't hesitate to ask for the manager in the department store to see if your business card, which advertises tutorial services, can be dispensed with the microcomputer cartons, or by the sales staff.

Tutor in the Use of Computer Applications

If you have any experience in the top ten popular uses of micro-computers, then you might extend the tutorial services in Option 1 to win a second and third meeting with your customers.

The ten most popular and significant uses of desktop micros appear to be:

1. Word processing
2. VisiCalc®
3. Mailing list systems
4. Data base systems
5. Accounting systems
6. Data-bank access systems
7. Instructional programs or systems
8. Graphics and art systems
9. Statistical systems
10. Process control systems

Each of these major systems or classes of programs causes the computer to obey a new set of commands, thus providing unique services to the user. Learning to operate even one of these systems can be the basis for an entire college course. Students may be able to use a word processing system after three hours of instruction, but they will not be able to perform more than a few of the elementary services that could be performed if they received your tutoring.

On the other hand, your student may only have $60 to spend, and your three hours of private instruction may be all that is wanted or needed to get started at the small business where he or she works. Therefore, be flexible in tutoring so that you can give three hours or thirty hours of instruction, to the limits of the student's needs. *Don't forget to show people how to use the manual that came with the software.*

The development of your own skills in several of these popular systems can be enhanced by taking evening classes at high schools, continuing education courses at colleges, or training through the hardware manufacturers' regional contacts, whose names can be obtained from computer store owners.

If you pay tuition when you take these courses, you may be eligible for tax deductions as you improve and maintain skills— depending, of course, on the manner in which you organize and conduct your business.

M. Ballard was pushed by her husband into offering a word processing service out of their home while he was at work all day. He bought an Apple® computer with disk and printer and expected her to get on with the business. After some despair and fear, M. called a private tutor and learned that they should buy a word processing package, a carbon ribbon for the printer, and several dozen disks. The tutor couldn't even discuss word processing until the second session because so many other basic issues had to be resolved.

Samples of microcomputer magazines related to word processing, accounting, graphics, etcetera, will be of interest to your clients. Loan them out, provide samples and encourage your clients to subscribe to them. (See Appendix A.)

Tutor in the Various Microcomputer Languages

BASIC is available on nearly all microcomputers when they are turned on. Bookstores are loaded with books on BASIC for each type of micro, and you can find ample books and guides to follow if you need to improve your own programming skills.

Fortunately for you, the manuals that come in the carton with the computer are generally inadequate (some would say terrible) for the new buyer.

Despite the thousands of books on BASIC and the courses offered in schools and colleges, and despite the relative simplicity of the language, wave after wave of new people appear who are just beginning to ask, "What does LIST do?" or "What does FOR I = 1 TO 10 mean?"

This relentless demand for tutoring is likely to continue at least through 1990. The lack of teachers is a great vacuum in the culture, and you can help to fill it. People pay willingly for this instruction, and not all of the students will grasp the concepts in the first three hours. A flexible approach is appropriate. People sign up for *private* tutoring, as opposed to group instruction, hoping that you will be more patient and flexible than the classroom teacher would be. Try to give the students what they need — personalized assistance.

Beyond BASIC, some people may be attracted to your services if you are competent to teach PASCAL, FORTRAN, Fourth, APL, Assembler, or other languages. Before you offer the service, you must have a curriculum plan, exercises, and teaching materials that both challenge and engage the student. These materials cannot be invented overnight, nor can they be lifted or stolen from other teachers. There is some front-end investment in the preparation of these materials, and therefore your hourly rate may be higher when you arrange the materials creatively.

Most experts agree that students should be taught to write *structured* programs from their very first experience. If you are a self-taught programmer, do not overlook the merits of this concept. Programs that look like spaghetti cannot be read or understood by the student, and in some cases the author cannot understand the code one week later. Structured programs are logically clear, readable, and maintainable. Your students will someday thank you for introducing them *from the start* to the concept of structured programming.

The book *A First Course in Computing*, by Arthur Luehrmann and Herbert Peckham, provides teaching materials that stress the concept of structured programming in micros. It is available from McGraw-Hill Book Company, 1221 Avenue of the Americas, New York, NY 10020.

Appendix F lists eight sources of workshop resources and curricular guides which can greatly speed your development of lesson plans or courses of study. Also, the user clubs listed in Appendix B will be of interest to your students. Show them the list.

Money Option 4

Consult on Resources and Options

Sometimes it's what you know. Microcomputers are extremely rich in service options, so if you have knowledge about software that does special things, or if you have wisdom about how to attach other devices to the micro, that knowledge can save other people *days* of research. Your clients should be glad to pay.

Every day people are asking questions like these:

- "What programs are available to give drill and practice to eighth graders on fractions and decimals?"
- "Which program should I buy?"
- "Where can I get programs that enable me to compose music at the micro keyboard?"
- "What features accompany each hardware system?"
- "If I buy this or that, will it do such and such?"
- "What micro should I buy next?"
- "How can I dial into the stock market and retrieve information for my portfolio to save on my microcomputer disk?"
- "How can I control my attic louvers and garage lights with my micro?"
- "How do I write programs that respond to light pens or joy sticks?"
- "How much would it cost to put a micro in every office of my company for word processing?"

These are typical of the questions asked every day. Some people, after asking long enough, will pay to get answers . . . *from you.* As your knowledge of micros builds and grows, it will be of value to others.

Since the microcomputer models change so rapidly, you will become a consultant if you merely collect information about prices and features. A list such as the one that follows can be a

12

tremendous asset to anyone who is about to purchase a machine. If you create your own list and include various features of each machine and the pricing on disk drives and printers, you will be able to assist people who want to discuss features and options. The price list was assembled in 25 minutes while I was touring the exhibit hall of the National Educational Computing Conference in Kansas City in June, 1982.

Popular Microcomputers and Prices[1]

Timex-Sinclair	3K Memory	$ 99 plus TV
VIC-20	3K	$199 plus TV
TI 99/4A	16K	$299 plus TV
Atari 400	16K	$350 plus TV
Radio Shack Color	16K	$399 plus TV
Commodore 64	64K	$599 plus TV
Atari 800	16K	$899 plus TV
PET	16K	$995
Apple II	48K	$1,530 plus TV
IBM	16K	$1,560 plus TV
Cromemco (with 1 disk drive built-in)	64K	$1,780
Osborne (with 2 disk drives built-in)	64K	$1,800
TRS80 Model III (with 2 disk drives built-in)	48K	$2,295

[1]Microcomputer prices change rapidly and readers should check periodically to keep up-to-date on latest prices.

Eighty-five microcomputer manufacturers introduced 100 new models of their machines at a recent NCC exhibition. That indicates the speed with which hardware is evolving, and implies that anyone who consults on hardware options must work to remain up-to-date. The chart which follows lists new hardware features which are likely to appear in the next few years.

Where Is the Microcomputer Industry Going?

- Flat lightweight screens that fold up and down providing high resolution pictures and graphics.
- Light pens that allow users to draw pictures on their screens.
- Voice output speakers that speak aloud the words appearing on the screens.
- Touch sensitive screens that allow users to point to desired items on the screen.
- Voice or sound input command systems that allow limited lists of words to be spoken *to* the computer, which it will obey.
- Stored repertoire of spoken words for the computer to speak to the user.
- Easy and low-cost plug-in connections to telephones and TV cable systems.
- Networking to other machines through the house wiring.
- Built-in page readers.
- Built-in printers.
- Teletex-compatible options.
- Ten million characters of disk type storage *within* the keyboard unit.
- One-fourth to one million characters of main memory within the keyboard unit.
- Holographic, three dimensional output from low-powered lasers.

Renting Your Microcomputer

If your microcomputer is simply laying in the closet unused, or if you have no interest in learning to use it, why not rent the computer system for profit? This won't bring you big money, but someone else who can't afford to buy a new computer may be pleased to rent it from you. If they like the equipment, they may eventually want to buy it.

Surprising opportunities for renting microcomputers abound. Tell the manager of a game and party store that you are willing to rent your machine. Fast food stores may also be interested. Music stores that rent band instruments also get requests for microcomputers.

Rent to Schools and Colleges

Both public and private institutions rent diverse services ranging from the pole lamps in parking lots to the band instruments in the music room. Equipment rental is part of the budget in almost all institutions.

Schools are struggling to make more microcomputers available to students and faculty, but just when they need to purchase more micros, they encounter declining enrollments and shrinking federal funds.

Colleges have, in general, moved more slowly than high schools in obtaining micros and are now trying to catch up. High school students are entering college asking, "Where are the micros?" They had better access to computers in high school than in college in many instances.

If your microcomputer has a tape recorder or disk drive, the system will have more value to the receiving school. Even if your micro has no disks or tapes, elementary schools may be interested in allowing children to "bang in BASIC" programs on it. Unadorned VIC-20®, Sinclair®, or Atari® computers are ideal for this use.

If you offer to rent your microcomputer system to a school, there are some key people to contact. The dean or principal may make the final decision, but it will probably be based on the recommendation of one of these people:

- The director of academic computing.
- A computer science faculty member or chairperson.
- A data processing faculty member or chairperson.
- A secretarial science faculty member or chairperson.
- A computer literacy teacher.
- A dean of instruction or school principal.
- A purchasing agent.
- The director of the computer center.

You can expect to rent your machine for monthly fees ranging from $5 to $60, depending on the disk or printer. Many schools pay $40 per month just for maintenance *on each micro-computer*, so if you release them from maintenance worries, they may be pleased to pay you $40 per month. Most schools have insurance to cover lightning damage and theft, so your computer may be covered better at school than it was at home. After a year or two of rental income, you will have recovered the cost of the equipment.

Schools and colleges often have laboratories with ten or fifteen micros lined up in rows. Your computer may be a welcome addition to their underequipped lab. Don't hesitate to call and ask. Otherwise they may have to spend $1,500 to $3,000 for a new microcomputer system. Your rental to them could be an answer to their cash-flow dilemma.

The Timex-Sinclair 1000 microcomputer is not much larger than the tape cassette standing behind it. Priced at $99.95, it was the first fully assembled computer to break the $100 price barrier.

Place Coin-Operated Micros in Libraries

Libraries are facing dreadful financial cutbacks, and many public libraries are about to close in bankruptcy. In order to remain solvent, libraries will gradually begin to charge for the services they provide. Coin-operated microcomputers are an ideal way for them to recover money for a public service. Your microcomputer could be placed on a coin-operated table where the incoming quarters (or dollars) will pay the library for their investment in the coin-operated computer system. These coins will also bring monthly income to you as the public pays to use your machine.

You can only qualify for this option if your computer system is fairly complete, containing a disk drive (not a tape unit). A printer is also helpful, but is not required.

Explain to the director of your local library that a Compuvend® coin-operated table can be obtained for about $1,950. You will then take your computer system (without charge) and bolt it to the coin table for the public to use. You will also provide some disks of software that the library personnel can dispense from their central desk.

The vend rate is typically set for fifteen or twenty minutes of time dispensed for each quarter deposited. Users can deposit up to fifteen quarters at a time to give themselves uninterrupted hours of use.

Librarians are provided with a master key so that they can use the system free of charge for themselves. Thus they can use word processing or financial packages during slow hours when the public is not demanding its use.

Everyone wins in this money-making option. The library advances $1,950 to purchase the coin-operated table, and that cost will probably be paid off in six to ten months. You might arrange to split the proceeds, with one-fourth to you and three-fourths to them until the table is paid off. After that, you could split the proceeds fifty-fifty. Income of $2,000 to $4,000 per year is possible for both you and the library.

Try to provide pleasant games and other interesting programs with your computer. Also, prepare a bold print manual of simple instructions to guide the users. The librarians will be pleased or dismayed with this new service depending on the amount of pleasure or frustration people experience as they use the system.

Don't expect the library staff to do all the work. If you are willing to show up once a month to pick up your proceeds, why not then enhance the equipment with more attractive software and improved instructions? That can be one of your selling points: You will help the library to order the coin-operated equipment, set it up, clean it occasionally (off hours), and make it a

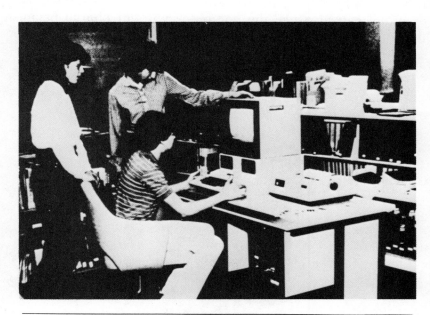

COMPUVEND COMPUTER EQUIPMENT VENDING SYSTEM SPECIFICATIONS
(All models, unless otherwise indicated)

Quarter Vend (Model 1310)
Dollar Bill Vend (Model 2110)
Token Vend (Model 3110)
Vend Override Staff Key
Adjustable Fixed Rate of Charge Per Unit of Time
Cumulative Time Capability
Multiple Equipment Usage
Dual Vend (Optional with all models)
Currency Deposit Light
Computer Equipment Ready Light

Flashing Light/Beeper Warning Signal
Two-Key Security System
Accounting Control System
100 Per Cent Solid State Circuitry
Power Source: 115V, 60 HZ, AC
Weight: 50 Pounds
Dimensions: Height 15"; Width 11.5"; Depth 15.25"
Rugged Steel Construction
One-Year Warranty

OTHER COMPUVEND PRODUCTS
Vend Computer Systems
Apple II Security Systems
Vend Tables

Call or Write:

CompuVend
COMPUTER SYSTEMS, INC.

5211 Oxford Avenue
Philadelphia, PA 19124
(215) 537-8291

P.O. Box 73
Williamstown, N.J. 08094
(609) 778-0566

Distributed by:

working unit—if they will advance the cash to buy the table. That way, they can offer a new service that will probably pay for itself within their fiscal year, and may even generate some profit.

Without your microcomputer, the library may not be able to advance $5,000 to buy a complete table with a new computer on it. Your offer of a micro to place on the table may tip the balance and make it possible. Remember, the coins pay for the table and also give you a monthly income. Call your nearest library for an appointment, show them the picture, and describe the opportunities they have for generating income. Don't forget, the library personnel can also use the computer without charge because they hold the master key.

The Compuvend Table offers two vending systems. Model 1310 operates on quarters and Model 2110 uses dollar bills. Both models provide up to 99 minutes of uninterrupted equipment usage without additional currency insertion. Each model features a unique cumulative system which allows the operator to insert up to 15 units of currency for a total of 24¾ hours of uninterrupted equipment usage. Both models include Vend Override Staff Keys that provide staff members with full use of the cumulative feature.

Libraries are always looking for new public services to offer to their patrons. You might therefore inquire about the possibility of offering weekly public instruction in the use of microcomputers. The library conference room makes an ideal classroom and all of the ideas about tutoring in Chapter 1 can be incorporated into library seminars. Introductory lectures in the library could give you visibility and credibility as a teacher. Your students in the library may become your paying students at home.

3

Writing Programs for Fun and Profit

25

Thousands of readers already know how to write programs in BASIC, and many of you have gone on to advanced levels of programming in various computer languages. But what success have you had in selling your programs?

A few software writers have earned more than a million dollars profit from their software sales, which shows that good software is valuable. Your programs may not be earth-shaking, but if you sell them you can earn a continuing royalty.

Jim Cutler always gave his programs away. People liked the clever graphics and simple tasks he accomplished in the programs. He wrote a program that would copy selected parts of one disk to another disk. He wrote programs to assist his children with their homework. People begged to get each new program—for free. Later the programs showed up in the public domain disks distributed nationwide by the microcomputer manufacturer. Jim will never get paid for his good work.

Some of the microcomputer user clubs (see Appendix B) have more than 3,000 public domain programs that are freely contributed by members. If 50 people contribute two programs twice a year to the club, the collection of free programs grows rapidly. But that doesn't mean that all club members give all their programs away.

Before 1973, computer hardware cost much more than the software that ran on it. After that year, with the dropping prices of computers and the escalating salaries of programmers, software began to cost much more than the hardware.

Today, the demand for software is so great that even with an estimated 3,000 people writing programs in their homes and selling them by mail order, the demand for high-quality programs (either business, educational, or scientific) will not be met for many years. New models of microcomputers are introduced annually, and the software becomes obsolete quickly as new options for sound, color, and graphics emerge.

Money Option 7

Sell Programs from Your Home

Cottage industry (people earning money while working at home) probably provides about one-fourth of the microcomputer software sold today. To get into this business, you simply advertise your software in microcomputer magazines and distribute flyers or catalogs that list and describe your software.

Appendix A lists the names and addresses of most of the microcomputer journals. You can advertise your software at very low cost in most of them.

Appendix C lists the home offices of many of the microcomputer manufacturers. Many of them publish catalogs of software that runs on their machines, and you could list your software in one of these vendor catalogs.

Appendix D lists various software directories that may be willing to list your software without any advertising fee. In Money Option 8 you will read about software agents who can assist the marketing of your programs in a professional manner. Their services go beyond the basement mail-order operation described here, but many people will want to try selling software on their own before calling the software agents.

If you are writing educational software, the educational software magazines are a good avenue for reaching potential buyers. Similarly, there are other journals for lawyers, doctors, churches, and small businesses.

Assuming you have a few original programs on hand, consider the benefits of setting up a business before advertising. Call a lawyer, get approval for your company name, and move toward incorporation. The setup costs may vary from $500 to $700, but the incorporation will allow you to deduct all legitimate costs and to bring your revenue into the company bank account.

You should probably have more than one program to sell, of course, and they should meet some minimal criteria if you are serious about earning money. Create a small catalog describing your programs, and in the descriptions show that the programs meet some or all of these standards.

Some of the basic requirements are:

1. The programs should be original. Don't attempt to rework

29

public domain software or to change tic-tac-toe programs just a little.

2. Instructions should be included within the software.

3. A manual or brochure should accompany each program.

4. Graphics, color, and sound should be used to advantage.

5. "YES-NO" and "STOP" replies should be handled consistently. "HELP" options should be provided.

6. All branching paths must be tested and made error-free.

7. Arithmetic results must be tested for accuracy.

8. The software listing and its manual should be copyright protected.

9. A variety of versions should be prepared, typically for Apple®, TRS-80®, Commodore®, IBM®, Atari®, and others. If you have both disk and tape versions of your programs you will increase your sales.

Three sales avenues exist. Magazines and journal ads are one avenue. Before placing an ad, however, you should send a press release or announcement about the software to selected journals. There is a good chance that they may publish your information in their new products column free of charge—an opportunity you should not pass up. Tell the readers to write for your free catalog. Appendix A is rich with these opportunities.

A second avenue for sales is to have your products listed in the various software catalogs. If your software runs on Apple and Commodore machines, for example, send your paragraph descriptions together with prices and titles to the vendors in whose catalogs you wish the programs to appear. (See Appendix C.) Six to twelve months may pass before they reprint their software catalogs, so you must be prepared to wait. DataPro, Auerbach, and dozens of other publishers print catalogs of software. Use them all to advantage—they provide free and respected software lists. (See Appendix D.)

A third avenue is the direct mail approach. If you wish to send a flyer about your educational software (for instance) to all school district directors of instructional computing, you can buy mailing labels at very low cost to target any desired audience. One such source specializing in educational mailing lists is:

Quality Education Data
P. O. Box 4507
Denver, CO 80204
(303) 572-8692

For mailings to small business owners, one mailing list firm is:

Edith Roman Associates, Inc.
875 Avenue of the Americas
New York, NY 10001
(212) 695-3836

For small, medium and large businesses, lists can be obtained from:

Dun's Marketing Services
Three Century Drive
Parsippany, NJ 07054
(800) 526-0665

Then comes the question of duplication. How will you copy your disks and tapes? You can make your own copies at home each evening, but if the orders come in twenty to forty per day, you won't be able to keep up. If you are trying to maintain versions for three or four types of equipment, you may want to hire out the task to firms that specialize in duplication. They advertise in most of the journals.

One company specializing in the duplication of cassette tapes is:

Microset Company
475 Ellis Street
Mountain View, CA 94043

Programmers who hope to rely on software sales for their primary income should probably invest in two excellent reference books by B. J. Korites. Mr. Korites is an experienced software writer and seller. His titles are: *Freelance Software Marketing: A Practical Guide to Selling and Licensing Proprietary Computer Software,* and *The 1980 Software Writer's Market,* which lists 1,800 places to sell software. The books are available

Radio Shack's TRS-80 Color Computer.

from Kern Publications, 190 Duck Hill Road, P. O. Box 1029, Duxbury, MA 02332.

The promotion and advertising of your software may cost as little as $20 for one-inch ads in the back of the microcomputer journals, or as much as $8,000 for a full-page color ad in an airlines magazine. You can write to any magazine of your choice requesting their advertising rate folder (no charge).

There are other ways to show your products to the public besides advertising. The book *How to Steal a Million in Free Publicity*, by Harry Barber, describes a host of clever ways of getting free advertising. It is available from Success Sellers, Box 16801, Irvine, CA 92713.

If you offer a moneyback guarantee with your software, you

will increase sales, but the risk of software theft by illegal copying increases as well. Good methods for software protection represent a sticky problem for which the industry awaits a creative solution.

Buyers usually wish that they had options for previewing or pretesting your software with a no-charge return to you if it doesn't fit their situation. To solve this, you could type on paper the significant screens or events your program generates and write documentation so fully that customers could commit to buying or not buying after seeing the written description.

Such documents should be submitted for copyright. Even so, somewhere a creative programmer may decide to code a new program that steals your idea—based on the super documentation you passed out freely to curious but unknown inquirers. Most solutions to this problem are a trade-off at best.

Money Option 8

Sell Software through a Book Publishing Company

If your software programs were distributed and sold by a publishing company, you would get royalties on the sales just as if you had written a book. Not everyone has experienced this process, so here is how it works.

Let's pretend you have written a book and a publisher has contracted with you to print, market, and sell it. Your contract will state that you are to receive a royalty of ten to fifteen percent of the wholesale price of the book every time it is sold. Thus, if the publisher sells your book to the bookstores for $5 each, the bookstore may sell it to the public for the price of $10. You would then get a royalty of 75¢ on each sale. A check would be written to you periodically for the accumulated royalties.

As an added incentive, publishers sometimes give you an advance on these royalties, typically amounting to $1,000 to $3,000 depending on the volume of sales they predict for the book. Publishers won't give more advance money than they expect to accrue during the first eight months after publication of the book.

Publishers are anxious to publish and sell *software* as well as printed materials, and they are looking for high-quality programs that supplement all types of subjects and disciplines. See Appendix G for a list of book publishers who carry software in their catalogs.

There are also many companies who publish only software (not books). These software publishing companies are listed in Appendix H.

How can you, the software author, make contact with these publishers? You can try it yourself, or you can work through an agent, who will demonstrate your software to the publishers' managers of software development and promote your programs to them.

The software agent typically charges twenty percent of your royalty up to some maximum such as $4,000 or $5,000. The agent can receive this money directly from the publisher as the royalties are paid over a period of time. The contract between you and the publisher can state this. Certain travel expenses may be added to the fee when you have approved such travel as appropriate and desired.

34

REWARD!

To anyone able to tame a TRS-80 or Apple program into a PET!!

I'm Wayne Green....I have a problem and I need your help. And, while helping me, you will be able to make some money to help you buy more computer equipment and programs. Got your interest?

There are three ways you may be able to help. First, I hope you are familiar with a new publication I'm putting out: *Desktop Computing*. This is the first totally non-technical computer magazine. It's designed for the average businessman or educator to let him know what small computers can do and what he should buy. Since 82% of the readers determine the computer purchases for their companies, it is an incredibly powerful group of readers. I would like to have as many articles on the business and educational uses for Commodore computers as I can get. The secret of writing for *Desktop* is to leave out all of the usual buzz words and computer terms. They really aren't necessary, as we've clearly shown with *Desktop*.

I also have a need for articles on Commodore computers for *Microcomputing* magazine. These should be aimed at people who have a computer, but who are not engineers. The articles should be about usable programs, extensions of the documentation, and anything else that will help Commodore owners to get more from their systems. Reviews of programs and accessories are of interest. Conversions of programs for other systems published in *Microcomputing* so they will run on the PET, CBM or VIC are of great interest for Commodore owners (and prospective owners).

I left the best part...the most fun (and most lucrative) to last. Oh, I pay for all articles accepted for publication...and pay well. I don't think any other maga-

zine beats me on that. But the big money, as you already know, is in software. Let me explain the situation.

Four years ago, suspecting that eventually there might be a need for packaged software, I started a small division of my publishing firm in the potato cellar of our 230-year old HQ building. It took us forever to get programs on the market so the obvious name was: Instant Software. Since that time freelance authors have submitted well over 10,000 programs for publication and Instant Software has it's own building. Of this number we've chosen about a thousand which we think have good commercial prospects if published. We have some 300 of these on the market, mostly for the TRS-80 systems, because there are so many of them.

The money for you, if you like to program, lies in taking some of these TRS programs and converting them so they will run on Commodore systems. We'll split the program royalties between you and the original author for this developmental work...which should be fun as well as income producing. You'll want to have access to a TRS-80 system for help in converting the graphics.

If this looks like something you'd be interested in drop me a letter and tell me what kind of programs you prefer: games, business, simulations, educational, scientific or utilities. Assure me that you have both a Commodore system and a TRS-80 at your disposal. Disks? Write to Wayne Green c/o Com-versions, Instant Software, Peterborough NH 03458.

If you are going to send in articles it won't hurt to send for our instructions for writing...Drop a line to Writer's Unblock, Wayne Green Inc, Peterborough NH 03458.

Instant Software

Peterborough, N.H. 03458 USA   A subsidiary of Wayne Green Inc.

Some large publishers receive 12,000 unsolicited book manuscripts per year. That's fifty every working day. And as many as 200 unsolicited software disks and tapes of all sorts may be received annually by just one publisher. A high percentage of these products are unrelated to the goals or interests of the publisher, and everyone's time is wasted — both the authors' and theirs. That's why you may prefer to work through a software agent even though you sacrifice a few dollars.

What if 200 software writers tried to call in advance to just one of the fifty software publishers to describe their programs? Publishers can't handle that many unproductive calls just to make a hit on two or three that might be money-makers for them. Unsolicited disks and tapes require publishers to write letters and conduct software evaluations. As you can see, the software agent is a perfect solution to this problem.

Take a look at the phone conversation in the illustration on page 37 and you will appreciate the problem that publishers face. You probably wouldn't make a call like that one, but some people do. Multiply this one by 200 calls per year, and you can understand why it begins to sound old to software directors at the publishing companies.

Software agents to the rescue. For the few dollars they charge, here is what they have to offer:

- Knowledge of the publishing companies and what type of programs they are willing to consider.

- Knowledge of competing products that are similar to or different from yours.

- Personal contacts at the publishing firms who are willing to listen and receive demonstrations from agents.

- Preevaluation services, helping you to make the product more presentable. Sometimes you may wish to pay extra for this service.

- Knowledge of the equipment lines (Apple, Texas Instruments, etc.) preferred by each publisher.

- Special demonstration skills acceptable to busy publishers.

- Knowledge of publishers' contract and royalty options.

11:00 A.M. The Phone Rings

Hello Ann? Are you the editor or director of software there at Jones Publishing? How are you today? I'm George.

I've got a little something here that I wrote—it's a program and maybe you should look at it. It only runs on Osborne equipment right now but I was thinking about converting it to run on Radio Shack and adding color later on—I've shown it to several people here and they all seem to like it—it's only 600 lines of code but I don't know—you people are the professionals and maybe you could look at it and see what you think because if it isn't worth anything I don't want to invest any more time in it but on the other hand if you thought it had potential then maybe I should go further with it—I could mail it—do you have an Osborne computer there? Because if you don't maybe a dealer could loan one to you.

It's a program that community fire houses can use when they coordinate bazaars or group lawn sales and we've tried it twice at the town strawberry festivals and also we have this ambulance coin-toss where money is coming in and the program does all the accounting and prints a couple of reports. Do you have something like that already?

People I talk to say that every community has need for something like this and if you are interested I could mail it as soon as I write some documentation and fix this one bug that we found happens everytime someone enters two-dollar bill donations.

Dr. Goldman who is a local dentist helped write part of the program so I don't own all of it but we could split the royalties or something.

You're not coming through here next week are you? Because we will have it all set up at the firehouse until Thursday, unless you wanted to come to my house on Friday.

Shall I mail it?

- Knowledge of documentation standards and publishers' requirements.
- Knowledge of software distribution packaging and distribution arrangements and how these are wired together.
- Knowledge of various options under which software writers incorporate, start home businesses, etc.
- Knowledge of foreign markets, trade markets, and other surprise markets that you might not consider.
- Knowledge of publishers who can market and distribute software more effectively than others.

James Allison mailed a creative new program to fourteen publishers each month for fourteen months. Each time, the publishers mailed it back, sometimes with notes that stated, "We cannot possibly review the hundreds of manuscripts and disks of software that arrive daily, and therefore we request that you submit your materials through an agent." The software was eventually purchased by a publisher, but many months were lost while it drifted around the country.

Unless a personal demonstration of your software can be provided to the publisher, the disk or tape containing the software may never be successfully viewed. Publishers may not have time to read your directions, and their equipment may be a different model, or the ROM level in their computer may be different from yours. Therefore a software agent may be the key to making contact with the right publisher. These agents know what types of programs are desired by the various publishers, and they know how to give professional demonstrations in a manner that saves time for all parties.

Sometimes the agent will notice that your software is not quite ready for demonstration, in which case the agent can assist you in refining the program so that it meets the standards the publisher requires. Most programs should use color and motion to advantage. Sound and graphics also add an extra dimension to the product. Instructions and restart options should be included.

Groups of three to ten related programs might be prepared so that they can be sold as a library of related programs. The agent would show them as a series, and your contract would cover the entire group of programs.

When you go to a publisher through an agent, confidentiality and security are fairly guaranteed. Agents earn continuing business and credibility by dealing with integrity in each transaction. They usually have a personal acquaintance with the publishers' directors of software, and they would discontinue contact with any publisher who was suspected of stealing or copying ideas from demonstration programs. Nondisclosure letters are a clumsy but final resort if you are worried about confidentiality.

The disk of software and the written description is not likely to be copied by anyone if the agent handles it personally. After the maximum royalties limit has been paid to the agent, he or she is out of the picture and does not share in future royalties. Appendix E lists selected software agents who are known by this writer to be industry-wise and reliable in past business dealings.

The diagram on page 40 deserves attention. If it seems complicated, then you should definitely work through an agent when selling your software.

How Software Gets to End Users

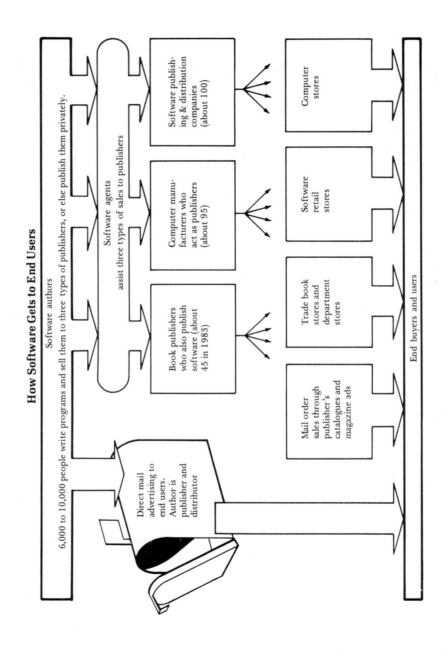

Software authors

6,000 to 10,000 people write programs and sell them to three types of publishers, or else publish them privately.

Software agents
assist three types of sales to publishers

Book publishers who also publish software (about 45 in 1983)

Computer manufacturers who act as publishers (about 95)

Software publishing & distribution companies (about 100)

Direct mail advertising to end users. Author is publisher and distributor

Mail order sales through publisher's catalogues and magazine ads

Trade book stores and department stores

Software retail stores

Computer stores

End buyers and users

Money Option 9

Sell Programs to a Computer Manufacturer

Apple, Radio Shack, Commodore, Atari, Texas Instruments, IBM, and many other microcomputer vendors sell selected software from within their corporate organizations. They get this software from three sources:

1. Their internal programmers write and produce some of it.
2. They purchase some of the programs by license arrangement from large software houses.
3. They sometimes purchase programs from people like you.

The variety of schemes that vendors work out with software authors is surprising and complex. Here is a list of software arrangements that vendors have forged with programmers at one time or another.

- The vendor may buy your program outright, with no royalty to follow, so that the program can be placed in a "public domain" pool of programs.
- The vendor may announce a new computer model and may hire programmers on a part-time or short-term basis to translate programs from earlier models to the latest model. (See the Wayne Green advertisement on page 35.)
- The vendor may help you to market your programs without paying you at all. To do this, they will list your software and your address in their software catalog, helping you to sell it from your home.
- The vendor may buy your software outright, returning a royalty to you as it is sold through their dealer network. This type of arrangement is similar to the publishers' contract in Money Option 8, and the advance on royalty is sometimes provided.

    This type of royalty arrangement can become a problem for the author because of the bookkeeping problems, which sometimes dirty the relationship. I know several software authors who received a sizeable advance against royalties, but even after three years they had never received a royalty check. Lawsuits followed, and then the accounting problems came to light. Some of the dealership stores to whom the software had been sold were now gone. Corporate accounting systems at the vendor's home office may or may not have tracked the sales accurately. The disks may have been copied and packaged at remote locations by part-time staff, and the count of copies made may not have been accurately recorded at times. When this type of case comes to court, the software author cannot prove that 50,000 copies of the program were sold, and the computer vendor's books may show that a mere 500 copies were packaged and sold even though 1,000 dealer stores appeared to have been stocked with the software.

- The vendor may send you to a book publisher with whom a joint relationship exists. If the publisher contracts with you to buy your program, it will be listed in the catalogs of both the publisher and the microcomputer vendor.

How can you make contact with these manufacturers? You can write to them at their corporate addresses, which are listed in Appendix C. A few will respond, while others will not respond for months for no particular reason. Therefore, the software agent looms as the best mediator between you and corporate bureaucracy; they are listed in Appendix E.

There's money in those lines of code. Friends and relatives may think that you are just fooling around in front of your glassy screen, but you can point to hundreds of people who have received over $50,000 in royalties from their software products.

If you want to see what the latest software looks like, or if you wonder what type of software is purchased by the publishers, the following conferences have exhibit booths where the publishers show off their latest programs. Write or call these organizations for locations and dates.

ADCIS
Association for the Development of Computer Based
   Instructional Systems
Western Washington University
Bellingham, WA 98225
(206) 676-2860

AEDS
Association for Educational Data Systems
1201 16th Street NW
Washington, D.C. 20036
(202) 833-4100

NCC
National Computer Conference
AFIPS 1815 N. Lynn Street
Arlington, VA 22209
(703) 558-3610

NECC
National Educational Computing Conference
305 Jesse Hall
University of Missouri
Columbia, MO 65201
(314) 882-8320

ACM
Association for Computing Machinery
1133 Avenue of the Americas
New York, NY 10036
(212) 265-6300

Conducting Workshops and Seminars

When you tutor people privately you don't need any public speaking expertise. However, to be a workshop teacher you must have more formal preparation in teaching and planning agendas for programs. People who lack teaching ability, or who do not command attention when explaining details to small or large groups, may wish to consider other money-making options.

There is money in this type of work, however. One publishing company recently distributed a brochure describing their workshops, which would be held in various cities across the country. They gave a toll-free phone number for inquiries and received 1,000 calls in a thirty-day period. There is an incredible demand for small-group workshops. People are willing to pay $75 to $200 for one- or two-day workshops provided they have assurance that useful materials will be distributed and that there will be some microcomputers available for them to use in a hands-on setting.

Once I attended a conference of the American Federation of Teachers, in which a speaker described a microcomputer seminar that was conducted periodically for teachers. The audience complained vigorously that they had tried repeatedly to get into such seminars but the courses were always filled. Hundreds of hands went up to confirm the problem. This demand for one- and two-day seminars is likely to continue as group after group emerges for training and skill enhancement.

When you picture yourself setting up a workshop for the first time, questions arise such as:

- Where to get *equipment* for everyone to use.

- Where to get an *audience*.
- Where to get a *room* or *auditorium*.
- Where to get a *curriculum*.
- Where to *advertise*.
- Where to get a workshop *disk* full of software for people to use.

Most of these questions will be answered in the five options for workshops that follow.

Money Option 10

Lead Small Group Training Seminars

Unlike private tutoring, small-group workshops provide instruction to groups—typically three to twenty people. The instruction may cover any of the subjects mentioned in the preceding chapters, such as basic computer operations, computer awareness, computer literacy, computer applications, computer languages, or microcomputer systems recommendations. If you do not have skills in any of these areas or if you are unsuited for teaching, you may wish to flip ahead to another option. Don't try to teach unless you are suited for it.

If the only microcomputer you can bring to the workshop is the one you own, then you should not invite more than three people, and the curriculum should allow these three students to rotate through alternating activities involving keyboard experiences, paper and pencil exercises, and tutorial experiences. Most people will not consider the experience to be worth $75 if they do not get at least two hours at the keyboard of the microcomputer. One computer for every two students would be a more appropriate ratio. Consider renting or borrowing a second computer if necessary.

What if fifteen micros are needed in order to handle thirty students? Several options are available to you, and they are not as costly as you might expect. One option is to contact the owners of computer stores within a large radius of your location. Many owners of microcomputer stores cannot properly satisfy the continuing requests of their clients for training and seminars. Remember, the computer store owner is in the hardware business and may not wish to hire teachers or give courses on a full-time basis.

If the store owner understands the nature of your workshop services and if you appear to be professional, he or she may be willing to provide microcomputers for your students, either free or for a small fee. If you invite the store clerks to attend your workshop and if you give ten minutes for the store owner to describe his or her services to the group, the owner may be more motivated to support you with equipment.

Another alternative is for you to hold the workshop at a location where ten (or fifty) microcomputers are already housed.

That location will probably be a high school, a middle school, or an elementary school. Colleges are not as likely to open their facilities to you, whereas public school facilities are often vacant and available on weekends. Consider the value of allowing up to three teachers from the host school to attend your workshop free of charge in return for the use of their microcomputer laboratory on Saturday. Promise the school principal that you will not disturb the existing setup and that you will provide all of your own demonstration programs.

Another option is to advertise a special workshop for persons who can bring their own microcomputer, requesting that they bring their micro along to the workshop site. This could mean lots of computers of a variety of makes and types, so be prepared! You will need about 20 heavy extension cords with multiple three-prong outlets. Each disk unit, computer unit and printer unit will draw 50 to 150 watts. That quickly multiplies up to 300 or 400 watts per student station, so try to avoid having room lights on the same circuit with the wall plugs.

If as few as eight people register, you can probably rent a

This microcomputer seminar was conducted in Wisconsin by the author with ten computers on the stage. Eight video monitors enabled 300 college teachers to see the demonstrations. Workshop materials are referred to in Appendix F.

hotel room for the day and still have profit after you pay for the room. Some hotels or motels will give you a free meeting room if you agree to bring the group to their restaurant for lunch or dinner. Other hotels may charge up to $150 for the day, but your tuition fee can be fixed to cover all expenses plus the profit you deserve.

Finally, you could arrange a special monthly workshop for all those people who are buying a low-cost VIC, Atari, or Sinclair microcomputer. Low-cost computers like these are portable, and the low prices enable you to advertise, "Buy your computer this Friday . . . Learn to use it Saturday." Students will come to the workshop with their keyboards under their arms, and your problem of finding machines for them to use is neatly solved. If your location is a school, perhaps the TV sets you need would be available for your use from the school's audio-visual department.

The handout materials you provide to the students will be one of the visible returns from their workshop fee. If you are not adequately stocked with such materials, check Appendix F for a good source.

Your lesson plans and handouts should reflect your ability to describe lesson objectives, plus your awareness of the journals and literature in the field. Curricular plans with lesson objectives are available in Appendix F.

Money Option 11

Conduct Classes in the Dealer's Showroom

Owners of computer stores often advertise their merchandise in the local newspapers and in flyers of all types. These store owners, in many cases, cannot offer training classes, software installation support, and general consulting. Buyers sometimes feel that a thousand dollars worth of support services ought to accompany their purchase of a $300 computer. The dealer knows better but is caught between being a nice guy or gal and being a nasty one.

Therefore, you might strike a deal with the store owner. Your reputation or experience as a successful tutor may convince the owner to allow you to become a workshop leader under the store umbrella. Three evening sessions could be arranged for workshops in the store, such as Thursday, Friday, and Saturday from 7 to 9 PM. You might limit the enrollment to eight or ten people and hold the class in the store display room, where the equipment gleams.

Split the tuition fees with the store owner in any equitable way, but remember that the store and the image it enjoys will be enhanced by the professional services you offer. If you make yourself useful, the store owner may want to hire you in marketing or sales support. Eventually you may deserve commissions on the extra hardware sales that result from the leads you produce and the hardware you recommend in your workshops.

Dealers usually have a collection of public domain software or demonstration programs for each of their computer models. If so, this can be an important source of software for your workshop disks. Your students will be pleased to have 50 to 100 programs on a disk for their "hands on" experimentation. If the dealer can't provide the software, you should write to the user clubs in Appendix B to obtain their public domain programs. Do not allow your students to copy your disks unless you are sure that every program on the disk is in the public domain. If you distribute proprietary software, whether intentionally or inadvertently, you may be liable for lawsuit—accused of software theft.

Several hundred public domain programs are also available

for the price of the disks by writing to: SWAPWARE, San Mateo Office of Education, 333 Main Street, Redwood City, CA 94063. Thirteen disks are available with versions for Apple, TRS-80, PET, and Compucolor computers.

Microcomputers are used uniquely in schools and colleges. Appendix I describes these uses in a structured way and you should be acquainted with it before teaching at the college level.

Teach Continuing Education Courses at Schools and Colleges

If you can lead workshops and seminars, you might consider branching out on a larger scale. Calls to any high school or college in your area will probably be productive. Ask for the director of the evening school, or in colleges ask for the director of continuing education. Your goal is to teach an evening course to adults entitled "Introduction to Desktop Microcomputers" or "Using Microcomputers in the Home or Office."

Specific application programs are popular with adult evening students. Therefore, you may be able to promise them that their course assignments will result in software that can be used in the gas station, hardware store, or other business area. The use of VisiCalc® or other accounting products will continue to attract adult learners for many years to come.

Colleges typically pay between $200 to $400 per credit hour, so you may received up to $800 for teaching about twenty eve-

Computer laboratories in elementary schools like this one could be used on weekends for adult workshops and seminars. Eighteen microcomputers are visible in the photograph. *Photo courtesy of Atari Corporation.*

ning classes. There will be other compensations besides money, however, and you will want to consider the trade-offs. In some cases, high school evening classes may be offered without any payment to teachers, but even so, they provide an excellent opportunity for leads and exposure to people who may be interested in your other services.

Money Option 13

Conduct Large Group Seminars or Speeches

The presentation of speeches about microcomputers and their future in our lives can be an exciting event for any public audience. Service clubs in most towns welcome local speakers if the theme is interesting and if the subject can be demonstrated or illustrated. Rotary Clubs, Lions, Elks, and other social and civic clubs are anxious to meet and recognize local agents who provide services to the community. Don't expect to be paid by the service clubs, but watch for leads to grow out of such speeches.

Depending on your skills as a public speaker, if you provide a captivating show to local or small audiences, larger opportunities will arise for speeches at banquets, conferences, and regional club meetings. You will not be able to charge for these services, however, until a few years of public speaking have developed your name and image. This money source cannot be tapped by everyone, but don't overlook its potential. Many paid speakers are quite boring, so if you find ways to be interesting in front of your audiences, you will eventually be able to ask $100 to $500 for entertaining or enlightening people at such gatherings as conferences or service club banquets.

Money Option 14

Start Your Own Franchised School

About fifty private computer schools are incorporated throughout the country, and some of them are franchised operations. If you have demonstrated competence as an administrator and if you have some capital to invest, the time may be right for starting a microcomputer school. Your school could provide training to children, adults, or both.

If your city already has a microcomputer school, don't try to compete unless your market research indicates that there is a continuing flow of students for both your school and theirs.

One way to organize and get started quickly is to franchise the name and materials of an existing microcomputer school. One such school is "The Children's Computer School." Founded by Dr. Eugene Galanter in 1980, the school has grown and now can be franchised in other cities. Dr. Galanter started this private enterprise as a service to the children and parents of New York City. His address is: Children's Computer School, 21 West 86th Street, New York, NY 10024 (212) 580-1335.

TUITION AND FEES

Children's Programs

The tuition fee for children's programming courses is $105.00 per eight hour module.

The Summer Session tuition (15 hours) is $210.00 .

The tuition fee for Special Children's Seminars varies. Please call the Registrar for course lists, schedules, and fees.

Adult Programs

The tuition fee for introductory BASIC programming is $105.00 .

The tuition fee for advanced programming courses is $145.00 .

Special Seminar Tuitions vary. Some current tuition fees for special seminars are:

WORD PROCESSING $105.00
DATA BASE MANAGEMENT ... $ 65.00
PLOTTER AND GRAPHICS $105.00
SPREAD SHEET PROGRAMS .. $145.00

COMPUTER RENTAL AND SALES

The CHILDREN's COMPUTER SCHOOL makes available rental computers for use by our students at home. The rental fee can be applied to the purchase of the machines. We can also provide our students with other computers and peripheral equipment, as well as commercial and proprietary software programs.

(CBM and PET are registered trademarks of Commodore Business Machines).

The Children's Computer School
21 W 86 St.
New York, NY 10024

THE CHILDREN'S COMPUTER SCHOOL

"YOUR CHILD (AND YOU!) WILL MASTER THE FUTURE"

5

Selling Out: What Are the Options?

59

Money Option 15

Sell Broken Machines for Parts

If your microcomputer is broken, and if you have no interest in repairing it, the parts may be of value to someone else who uses that particular model. Some people are content with their first computer, which they may have bought in 1977, for instance, and they may be determined to keep it running on into the twenty-first century.

Such tinkerers and devoted hobbyists read the fine print carefully in several microcomputer magazines. If you place an ad in one of these journals (see Appendix A), you may be pleasantly surprised to receive responses from people who offer $50 to $300 for the parts contained in your broken machine.

Assuming the machine works, when you write a sales ad give the readers some assurance that the machine has never been crushed, dropped in salt water, nor struck by lightning. If your microcomputer was damaged by lightning that came down the powerlines, don't try to sell it. It's probably worthless. If an expert has told you that one 4K memory chip is bad, or in other ways has explained any problems, your ad might mention this for the reader to appraise. A sample ad might read:

FOR SALE: TRS80 MOD II MICRO WITH CASSETTE DRIVE AND PRINTER, 21 PGM. TAPES AND T.V. MONITOR. POWER CABLE MISSING, OTHERWISE OPERATIVE.

Computer dealers are not likely to be interested in your broken machine, but they may be able to refer you to other people or schools who own equipment like yours. They will usually know about local or regional user clubs, too. These clubs can post your "For Sale" message on their bulletin board. (See Appendix B.)

Local drug stores or small convenience stores often carry "Buy, Sell, Swap, Trade" magazines or newspapers at the checkout counter. Before advertising your broken computer in national journals, you should list it in local papers to see if people in your area are interested.

Remember that a broken computer, like a broken TV set or a

broken watch, may be valuable or worthless depending on the extent of damage and the needs of the beholder who matches his working system to your parts and pieces. No one asks full value for a broken toaster, microwave oven, or typewriter, and you should not expect to reap a bonanza from a broken computer.

Just as you would wax a car before showing it to the car salesman for trade-in, consider whether you should have your computer repaired or cleaned before trying to sell it. It will be worth a lot more money if it works and looks good.

Money Option 16

Trade in Your Older or Unused Microcomputer

Just as you might trade in your washing machine to reduce the price of a new one, some computer dealers are willing to accept old microcomputers as a trade-in. Don't forget to ask them.

The day is coming, however, when trade-in allowances will vanish for most used computers unless they are higher priced business systems in the higher price categories. Eventually home computers—with ever more flashy features and ever lower prices—will evolve so rapidly that home buyers will be able to buy *complete* systems with disk and printer for less than $1,000. As computer costs keep falling, older models will be regarded as throwaway units after one or two years of use.

Until then, however, your local dealer may be able to take your old computer as a trade-in, so don't hesitate to ask. Dealers report that about ten percent of the public buyers have an older computer to trade in.

Money Option 17

Sell Your Microcomputer Outright

Assuming that your computer is in working order, several avenues of sale are open to you.

1. Companies that specialize in used computers may buy it.
2. Computer clubs may advertise it.
3. You can try "Buy, Sell, Swap, Trade" advertising.
4. National magazine advertising may prove effective.
5. You may contribute equipment to a school with a tax write-off.

There are a number of companies that handle used computers for people who wish to sell equipment quickly and effortlessly. Like the bluebook value of a used car, you will settle for whatever price the dealer offers. It may not be your hoped-for price, but the sale will be quickly settled. Consider these dealers:

COMPUCHANGE
Box 4151
Anaheim, CA 92803
(714) 535-1990

THE PROCESSOR (Magazine)
Box 518
Webster City, IA 50595
(800) 247-4800

COMPUTER TRADER
1704 Sam Drive
Birmingham, AL 35235
(205) 854-0271

Advertising your used computer at a *local computer club* is an excellent way to sell equipment. Start with clubs within a fifty-mile radius of your home. To find them, you should call the computer stores listed in your yellow pages, asking them how to contact the clubs. Such user clubs exist for nearly all of the popular machines, such as Apple, Radio Shack, Texas Instruments, Commodore, Atari, and Sinclair.

A listing of national user clubs is available at the back of this book for those who wish to examine it. The list is updated from national vendor lists. (See Appendix B.)

Swap-and-sell advertising was described earlier. The sample ads below are typical of the type found in such magazines and papers, circulated in most regions of the United States. Payment for the listings is often contingent on sale of the goods. Regional and city newspapers are also good places to advertise computer equipment. Some newspapers accept ads by telephone, which

HOME COMPUTERS VIDEOS

Radio Shack Acoustic Modem (telephone interface II) w/ cable, $75. Call 269-

Radio Shack TRS 80 computer Mod. I, Level II, 48 K RAM w/ expansion interface, has books, manuals & some programs, $600. Call

Radio Shack color computer, 32 K-Ram, extended basic, comes w/ 4 program packs, books, manuals & joysticks, $500. Call

Video games, Alien Invaders, port. units, needs minor repairs. Call aft. 6 pm.

Atari video game w/ all controls plus 14 tapes, $375. Call 933-

Atari game & 11 tapes, exc. cond., all for $250. Call

Sanyo video cass. recorder w/ tapes, current model, 5 mos. old, $425. Call

Must sell - Quasar video recorder w/ 7 tapes, $249. Call 383

HOME COMPUTERS & VIDEO EQUIPMENT 37

TELETYPE KSR-33 w/stand, plenty of paper incl, LN, $715; 677

VIDEO game w/ tennis, hockey, squash, shooting, VGC, $25; 878 aft 7pm

HITACHI VKC 800, w/warr, saticon tube, quality camera, $1075; 884

SONY KP7220, 6', 2pc, projection tv, w/ new flr or wall mnt screen, LN, $2400; 356

DYNAIR mini-fade, mdl VS220A, can fade & mix bet 2 cameras or video sources, EC, $225;

RADIO SHACK home computer, mdl 1, level II 48K, disc dr, all types of access, GC, $1500*;

JVC 6700U, 7 mos, fast forward, slow mo, still frame, auto indexinn. 2 wk programm-able, $600;

DISC player, CED by RCA w/1 disc, LN, $275;

FIDELITY voice sensory chess computer, o.b.o., w/case, LN, $180;

COLECO telstar video arcade w/4 carts & extra controls in orig box, LN, $85*;

PRINTER GE termi-net 300,80 cols, upper & lower case, 300 band, serial interface, VGC, $200;

HITACHI 9700 remote control home quad deck, $1140;

HITACHI 6500A port w/warr, $1075;

ATARI, 6 mos, incls space invaders, astroids football, combat, $140;

SELECTIVE output or home computer AJ 841 typewr, EC, $625;

BERKELEY universal freq counter & timer, $35;

INTELEVISION game w/4 cart. 3 wks, EC, $300,

INTELEVISION, master coponent, still in box, plus 5 game cart, $375* aft 5pm pe

RADIO shack, computer mdl 1,48-K memory, 2 disk drives, tax, stock, hull game, software, LN, $1500; aft 6pm pe

HAND held b&w video cam, zoom lens, 2/3 vidicon, NMR, $125;

TELSTAR coleco t.v. game, tennis, hockey, handball, 3-spds, 1 or 2 players, $13;

ATARI video games, console, 16 best carts, 2 storage cases, 1 extra joystick, warr card, 2 mos, LN, $385;

ATARI home video center, 3 carts, blk jack, circus & combat, VGC, joystick NMR, $85;

TRS 80 computer, 4K, mdl 1, incls video, keybrd, cass recorder, tbl bks, programs, LN, $475;

CREATIVE computing software tapes, (4), for pet computer, total 18 programs, $28;

ATARI video game, less than 1 yr, 11 carts, ce hockey, asteroids, etc, all access, EC, $275,

AXIOM EX800 electrostatic printer + 12 rolls of paper & manual, has parallel inter-uce, VGC, $175*;

SWTPC MP-A processor card, EC, $80*; bet 10-2, pa

2 DEC writer LA30 printers + documen-tation, has parallel interface, VGC, $400* or ses;

SWTPC C1b4 termina! + G16144 graphics board, + 12" B/W monitor, EC, $300*;

ELECTRONIC calculator, LN, $80;

EQUIPMENT rack on castors, 24"Wx 27"Dx62"H w/hinged rear dr & sides, VGC, $65*;

PERCOM LFD 400, disc controller card plus software (BASIC EO-ASM & other), EC, $150*;

JVC ¾" video player, mdl JVC-5000 auto repeat, VGC, $500;

ATARI home video game w/4 game carts & 3 sets of controls, LN, EC, $225;

ELECTRONIC TV, unisonic 6 games incl rifle & target, $23*;

ATARI cartridges, (5), space invaders, etc, $60,

TRS 80 color computer, hooks to any TV, incl cass recorder, personal finance program, learning lab, $495*;

VIDEO mach, peavey 1000, panasonic, 2 & 4 hr tapes, EC, $400,

TIME lapse videotape recorder, 48 hrs (or one hr) concord VTR-648, panasonic EC, $385,

VIDICON tube, 2 ope 20, same as 8929, 2 ope 19 or 4848 hitachi make, LN, $20;

BURROUGHS crt terminal, ndl TD820, composite video out put, RD-232, printer & modern connectors, EC $200;

HEWLETT-PACKARD hp 1300A X—Y monitor 20 MHZ bandwidth, 13" diag screen, LN, $1200;

SETCHELL-carlson 19" video monitor, hi resolution, B&W, EC, $75;

HITACHI VTR mdl SV—510D, elec editing, B&W to reel, new heads, EC, $195,

HITACHI "frame grabber" disc recorder /video maonitor, store & display one frame video, LN, $600;

VIDEO monitor conversion kit, converts sony tv to professional quality monitor/ rcvr, LN, $135,

SONY video monitor/rcvr, 8" B&W, programes GC, TR/computor, EC, $100;

RGB color video monitor 13", digital or analog input-computer or camerao, LN, $450;

VIDEO monitor, 9 hitachi hi resolution composite video, LN, $100;

WAVEFORM monitor, tektronix 527, EC, $400;

FLIM FLAM game, ping pong type game, 2 or 4 players, takes quarters, tbl type game from bar, LN, $250;

Microcomputer sale ads from "Swap and Sell" magazines.

simplifies your work. Some people state their selling price in the ad.

Here are some national computer magazines that may be willing to list your ad:

Datamation
666 5th Avenue
New York, NY 10103

Computerworld
Box 880
375 Cochituate Road
Framingham Road, MA 01701
(617) 879-0700

Computer System News
333 E. Shore Road
Manhasset, NY 11030
(516) 829-5880

Infoworld
530 Lytton
Palo Alto, CA 94301
(415) 328-4602

A list of microcomputer journals is presented in Appendix A. The list is larger than you need for selling your equipment, but it may be of interest.

Money Option 18

Donate to Charity

Why not consider giving your unused or outdated equipment away to a school or church, then enjoying the tax breaks from your charitable contribution?

This option is similar to a furniture donation to the Salvation Army. You must have your computer equipment appraised by an independent expert who gives you a letter stating the assessed value of the equipment. Your local computer store may be willing to provide the assessment letter.

After you have received the assessment statement, you should call the principals of schools in your neighborhood within thirty days, to see if they are willing to receive your contribution. Your total working system goes to the school (or church), and then you can mark the assessed value on the tax contribution form. A copy of the assessment statement must accompany the tax form.

Be sure that the items of equipment you give to the school are identical to the list of items on the assessment statement. Show the written statement to the receiving school and obtain a letter from them that lists equipment received. The two lists must be identical. Attach them both to your tax return.

In summary, you won't get wealthy from these sales, but if you want out of a mistaken or uninteresting set of equipment, you may as well try to get something out of it.

Setting Up Microcomputer Applications for Profit

*T*urkey or *turn-key*? Small business owners sometimes buy a microcomputer that is advertised as a turn-key system. Like turning a key, when the owner turns it on and obeys the instruction manual, it is supposed to do word processing, accounts receivable, or some other business application.

When I walked into a small business the other day, the owner said to me, "I have a micro upstairs and the accounts receivable stopped working two months ago. We're really in trouble. Do you know what I should do? It's a turkey."

If you have experience in the use of any of the popular microcomputer applications, there are at least three ways for you to earn extra money: fixing, advising, and designing.

Money Option 19

Fix or Diagnose Failing Application Systems

There seem to be an infinite number of wrong notes a beginner can find in a violin, and similarly a dentist, accountant, clergyman, or vice president may find cracks in a computer package that no amount of "idiot-proofing" could protect against.

These users are not dumb or malicious. They are simply unable to devote time to reading manuals or diagnosing errors that may appear. Data may be entered incorrectly. Or the meaning of computer terms such as, *account, record, transaction, file, subaccount, reading,* or *writing,* may be misunderstood by the user. Terms that the business user has always known now take on new and clouded meanings.

Sometimes these misconceptions do not cause trouble until one week, a month, or a year later. Quarterly or annual reports often flush out these problems, and not being able to give full attention to them, the small business owner may chuck the computer aside, praying that some angel from heaven will appear to set things right.

You can be that angel if you have proper experience and the courage to sell yourself as an expert.

Don't forget that silly or trivial things can bring an entire operation to a standstill—a loose or intermittent power cable, a pinched disk cable, dust in the disk drive, read or write errors, a stuck key on the keyboard, a key that transmits a different letter than the one that shows, and on and on. You never know what problem you will face until you get there.

Charge for your work by the half day so that the owner isn't frightened by the prospects of super consultant fees. Normal fees for this service might range from $150 to $450 per day provided you truly know what you are doing. If you can get the mailing lists rolling again, or the word processing or accounting system back in working order, you deserve fair pay.

Consider your liabilities as well, and avoid fooling around with systems you don't understand. If you wipe out a critical file or if the printer stops working after you leave, the owner may expect you to pay him. Experience makes the difference, so only sell yourself into situations where you can honestly be of help.

Money Option 20

Advise Clients About System Options

About ninety-five manufacturers produce microcomputers, and more than 2,000 complex software packages (each with ten to 100 programs) exist for schools and businesses. The confusion caused by this proliferation of software is not only bewildering, it is often unmanageable for the person who wants to buy into a particular system.

For example, the figure on page 73 shows the business functions a small school or college can implement on microcomputers. For some of these application areas, three to twenty packages could be purchased from various catalogs and software houses around the country. A similar list could be composed for institutions other than schools.

The portable Osborne microcomputer retails for about $1800 including two disk drives and small display screen. Teachers and traveling professionals regard its portability and low price as attractive features. *Photo courtesy of Osborne Computer.*

A buyer may want to know whether to buy IBM or Apple equipment, whether to buy a dot matrix or letter-quality printer, whether to get a color or noncolor screen, or whether to design and write software in-house or buy packaged software from catalogs.

Where can a buyer get information when a complex or costly system is contemplated? Questions about the options and the design of files or programs may go beyond the knowledge of the local dealer, and, if you are competent, the dealer may refer these questions to you. You would then operate as a private consultant, comparing the design of several different systems and helping the client to select wisely. The money saved by the client in not making false starts and taking wrong directions should pay your fee and prevent costly restarts.

Some system choices may require days of discussion and demonstration. Advice from an expert can make the difference between money well spent or poorly spent, a software package that fits or doesn't fit.

There is another level of advice to think about—the set-up process. What is the best way to set up a VisiCalc® financial reporting system or a general ledger account structure? How does one organize mailing lists for maximum efficiency?

A profession known as "datagrammer" may be recognized when enough people see the opportunity of setting up VisiCalc® reports and charts. If you could walk into an office with fifty or 100 layouts of VisiCalc®-type screens or files, you could review them with the owner, quickly cutting through costly trial-and-error experiments to a full and final working system. Aspiring datagrammers are potentially as valuable (and rewardable) as programmers, and their services will come to be recognized as necessary in the start-up process of such systems.

Business Applications Using Computers in Educational Institutions

Student Systems
  Admissions Records
  Pretest Records
  Student Scheduling
  Class Scheduling
  Student Curriculum Analysis
  Financial Aid Records
  Student Attendance
  Student & Class Reporting
  Grade Reporting
  Historic Data Base
  Bus Routing
  Commendation/Deficiency
  Transcripts
  Compensatory Education
  Course Catalog Preparation
  Faculty Load Analysis
  Student Registration
  Enrollment Reporting
  Degree Auditing

Financial Systems
  Accounts Receivable
  Accounts Payable
  General Ledger
  Budget Preparation
  Budgetary Accounting
  Planned Program Budget
  Cost Accounting
  Donation Accounting
  Construction Accounting
    & Auditing
  Capital Inventory
  Financial Aid Awards
  Fee Assessment
  Cash Collection
  Financial Planning & Modeling
  Grant & Research Accounting
  Depreciation Accounting
  Parking Lot Accounting
  Dormitory Accounting
  Payroll
  Purchasing & Encumbrance
  Bookstore Inventory & Accounting
  Stores & Revolving Inventory
  Space Utilization & Assignment
  National Defense Loan Accounting

Personnel Systems
  Position Control
  Staff Database with Resumés

Library Systems
  Book Circulation
  Book Acquisition
  Information Retrieval
  Budget Control

Public Relations Systems
  Mail List Management
  Alumni/Donation Records
  Employment Opportunity
  Parking Decals
  Theater Ticket Production
  Promotional Campaigns
  Direct Mail Campaigns
  Alumni Development

Counseling Systems
  Career Planning
  Placement
  College & Graduate
    School Searching
  Student Grant Searching

Administrative Aids
  Word & Text Processing
  VisiCalc®
  Slide Preparation System
  Phone Billing System
  Key & Lock Accounting
  Physical Plant Work Orders
  Safety Equipment Maintenance
  Phototypesetting & Printing
  Announcement System
  Electronic Mail System
  Faculty Conferencing System
  Secretarial CAI Training System
  Administrative Calendar
    Scheduling
  Statistical Graph Preparation
  Institutional Research
  Cohort Group Tracking
  Vehicle Scheduling & Tracking
  Statistical Analysis Systems

Install Database Systems

When your clients cannot afford to pay big money for specialized programs written just for them, they may still be able to get the results they want if you are able to demonstrate a database package to them.

Database packages can be purchased for prices ranging from $50 to $5,000. Such computer packages are usually run in either of two modes—set-up or production.

Since your client may not know how to handle the set-up mode, you can sell your services for an hourly fee. Since you might only work three to ten hours, the cost is low for your client and your commitment to the project is shorter than it would be for a programming project.

Some of the common database packages are listed in the chart on page 75 as they are advertised in many of the journals. These systems come with manuals and instructions, allowing you to respond to questions at set-up time. Your task is to state (once) to the database system those records the user wishes to place on disk, the length and type of each field in each record, and the format of the screen the user wants to use when entering data. You may also supply some parameters for producing printed reports.

Once you hammer out the answers to all the questions, the database package will remember the answers and freeze the system in the style you created.

The client can then run the package in production mode for many years to come. A menu screen usually asks the user whether he or she wishes to enter data, print reports, sort files into new sequences, and so on. The user can handle the application somewhat as a button pusher after you have set it up.

Later, if more features need to be added to the system, you may be called back to extend or improve the package. Such systems are especially useful in research labs, churches, clubs, and small businesses.

The JINSAM™ database package is an example of a popular database system that operates on IBM and Commodore microcomputers. The versatility of the database concept can be seen in the users of Jinsam, which includes NASA, a band booking com-

Popular Database Packages for Microcomputers

AIDS III
(TRS-80)
Meta Technologies
Euclid, OH 44132

ASERT
(Commodore)
CFI
875 West End Avenue
New York, NY 10025

Business DataBase System
(TRS-80, TI 99/4)
Charles Mann & Associates
7594 San Remo Trail
Yucca Valley, CA 92284

CCA Data Manager
(TRS-80)
Personal Software
Sunnyvale, CA 94088

Create-A-Base
Micro Computer Inc.
1520 E. Mulberry
Fort Collins, CO 80524

**Cromemco Database
   System**
Cromemco Inc.
280 Bernardo Avenue
Mountain View, CA 94043

Data Bank
(CP/M)
Software House Inc.
695 E. 10th North
Logan, UT 84321

Data Organizer
CMS Inc.
(TRS-80)
3132 N. Broadway
Chicago, IL 60657

DBMS
(Apple)
High Technology Software
8001 N. Classer Boulevard
Oklahoma City, OK 73113

Flex File
(Commodore)
AB Computers
252 Bethlehem Pike
Colmar, PA 18915

IDM-V
(TRS-80)
Micro Architect Inc.
96 Dothan Street
Arlington, MA 02174

IFO
(Apple II and III)
Software Technology for
   Computers
PO Box 428
Belmont, MA 02178

INFO-80
(Z80 CP/M)
The Software Store Ltd.
706 Chippewa Square
Marquette, MI 49855

JINSAM
(IBM, Commodore)
Jini Micro-Systems Inc.
Box 274 Kingsbridge Station
Rivervale, NY 10463

The MANAGER
(Commodore)
Canadian Micro Distributers
   Ltd.
365 Main Street
Milton, ONT L9T 1P7

Maxi Micro Manager
(TRS-80)
Adventure International
Longwood, FL 32750

Micro-Seed DBMS
(Z80 CP/M)
Microsoft Comsumer
  Products
400 108th Street Northeast
Bellvue, WA 98004

OZZ
(Commodore)
Commodore Business
  Machines
487 Devon Park Drive
Wayne, PA 10017

REQUEST
(TRS-80, Apple II, etc.)
United Software of America
750 Third Avenue
New York, NY 10017

SELECTOR IV
(Apple, CP/M)
Micro-Ap Inc.
7033 Village Parkway
Dublin, CA 94566

pany, the IRS, an Aruba gambling casino, a tuxedo store chain, various libraries, oil well companies, many educational institutions, and more. The package even allows users to run statistics programs against their files to obtain statistical charts and graphs.

Training in the use of these systems can be obtained by signing up for a database course at a community college or by buying your own package and setting up a sample system for yourself so that you know how to use it.

For a system which you could use around your own house, you might set up a locator system for music on your record albums or an inventory system for any collection that you have. Such experimental systems lead you into the process of defining just what you want the system to do. Later, children may find pleasure in entering the data after you have the system established and running. For example, after several months of entering data, you would be able to ask for a listing of all music classified as "country" recorded after 1981, including the number and name of the album on which it can be found. Or, any other strange request of your choice can be handled just as easily.

Money Option 22

Design Application Systems

When someone needs a set of programs to manage a doctor's office or to give drill in seventh-grade fractions, they can usually buy these programs for less money than it would cost to write them—unless appropriate programs simply can't be found. Maybe your client is insisting on software that is designed especially for a particular situation. If the client can afford customized software, you can earn money by designing a new system exactly matching the need.

That doesn't mean that you have to write the programs yourself; you can hire the coding task out to other people if you wish. But before programming begins, the system must be designed. A list of about 300 questions should be asked during this assessment of needs, and good system designers know the questions intuitively.

- How many files will best serve the user?
- What data elements are required in each file?
- How many programs will comprise the system?
- Can a data base management package be used with it?
- Should some of the reports provide input to word processing files?
- Who will own the resulting package?
- Will you be free to market it to others?
- What hardware will be recommended?
- What language should be used for writing the programs?
- Should the CPM® or other operating system be used?
- What reports are desired?
- What methods and cycles of data entry will be used?

Your work as a system designer should command good pay because decisions made at this level set the stage for the programming, the data entry, the cycles of operation, the method of file backup, the report capability, and the reliability of the system. If you do your designing job well, the system may have a three- to ten-year life.

Be sure to estimate carefully the cost of the effort and the time of delivery. Don't underestimate the scope of the task. One teacher obtained $800 as a summer stipend, promising to deliver thirty programs, which together were to comprise a system. Three summers later the job was still not complete, and a semester sabbatical was required to finish up the job.

Therefore, don't tackle a big system unless the client is fully aware of the scope and cost of the effort. Most people can have a program running in about twenty-five minutes. Then comes cleanup, graphics, testing, and integration with the other programs. Twenty-five days later it may be finished. Experienced programmers know this and will therefore estimate the cost of each job very carefully.

7

Connecting Micros to the World (for Hardware Buffs)

Several years ago *Popular Science* magazine ran an article on "Breslin," which described how an entire house was operated and cared for by a microcomputer.[1] Standing in any room or in the back yard, the owner could speak to Breslin, giving verbal commands such as "Outdoor lights on" or "Barbecue off." The computer would then answer with a computer voice, assuring that the command had been executed. Once in a while Breslin would decide to lock people out of the house, but not often.

The ability of the microcomputer to watch over thirty or a thousand circuits, circling through all of them every one or two seconds and making decisions about them, is a dazzling feat. The speed of the computer to flash through a list of instructions makes the control of space vehicles and robots possible.

In fact, rocket technology has existed since 1924, but we could not orbit the earth nor land on the moon until computer technology advanced sufficiently to calculate rapidly changing speeds and altitudes so that thrusters and rockets could be fired in precisely timed sequences. The microcomputer on your desk can probably calculate more than one million additions per second or any other function you set it to do. Some micros have provisions for the attachment of other devices to the computer, such as lights, switches, timers, motors, thermometers, and clocks.

Not many people do this, however, even though the idea of controlling attic louvers or furnace dampers or turning fans on and off in accordance with inside and outside temperatures is a

---

[1]Hawkins, Bill. "Breslin—The Home Computer That Runs My House." *Popular Science,* January 1980, pp. 82–84.

definite attraction. Most people aren't equipped with the technical skills needed to hook up motors or write programs to suit these situations.

The Commodore PET® and CBM® computers actually come with a plug in the back for attaching these types of controls. It's called the IEEE-488 channel. On Apple and Bell & Howell computers, an electronic circuit board can be purchased which adds the IEEE option to the machine. Other computers also have provisions or add-on options for controlling one's environment with the microcomputer.

The next sections describe three money options available to hardware buffs who understand how to hook appliances and other possessions to the IEEE (or other) channels micros provide. All three of these options can operate at two levels: (1) Attachments are purchased and, for a fee, you hook them up to the devices; and (2) you design attachments for special purpose situations that may or may not be available on the open market. Either way, there is money in this area for people who are handy with a soldering gun and who understand digital electronics.

Several useful books describe the technical aspects of the IEEE channel. Look for them at the local computer stores. One such book is PET Interfacing, from Howard W. Sams and Company, 4300 West 62nd Street, Indianapolis, IN 46206. This book provides technical information regarding the various pins, voltages, and functions that are used with the IEEE channel.

Another valuable reference book is Channel Data Book, available from Channel Data Systems, 5960 Mandarin Avenue, Goleta, CA 93017. This book lists hundreds of hardware attachments sold by various vendors to micro enthusiasts. Most of these attachments require some knowledge about how to attach them to the microcomputer in a reliable and useful way.

Thus, whether you design circuits or use circuitboards designed by others, there is money to be made in this area. I know one person in New England whose entire income is obtained from his knowledge of the IEEE channel and how to connect a world of devices to it.

Money Option 23

Build or Install Helpful Devices for the Home

The services of "Breslin" cannot be bought ready-made at present. Some useful things can be done, however, which are easily within the reach of current microcomputer technology. Most of us just don't know how to do it, so we rely on skilled hardware buffs to do it for us—and we pay.

Here are some attachments that could be sold to people:

- *Thermometers* that are continuously watched by the microcomputer in various places about the house—both indoors and outdoors—with the computer adjusting heat sources and fans accordingly.
- *Lights* and *switches* controlled by the micro.
- *Ham radio* connections to the micro.
- *Motors* turned on or off by the micro.
- *Model trains* or *airplanes* controlled by the micro.
- *Music synthesizers* and *music filters* controlled by the micro.
- *Clocks* and *timers* controlled by the micro.

Money Option 24

Assist School Teachers with
Their Computer Connections to Other Devices

Schools use microcomputers in so many diverse ways that it is difficult to state their needs. I observed a psychology class that had a pig in a small pen. The microcomputer would flash lights of different colors for various lengths of time. Sensors taped to the skin of the animal were sending signals to the computer continuously and being reported on a computer printer every five minutes, day and night. The sensing devices were designed just for this special experiment, and unique programs were written to collect and report the data. (See Appendix I.)

Here are some of the attachments that schools use or may wish to use if you show them how:

- *Light pens* that can draw on the TV screen.
- *Speech output devices.* The words on the computer screen are spoken aloud by the computer through a loudspeaker.
- *Joy sticks*—two or four of them at a time.
- *Voice input devices.* Commands spoken by the user are received by a microphone and interpreted by the micro.
- *High resolution graphics* and *screen plotting devices.*
- *Plotters* using pen and paper.
- *Music boards* and *multiple synthesizers* with professional music composition systems.
- *Connectors for attaching TV monitors to microcomputers* so that large audiences can see the screens.
- *Robot devices* and *"Turtles,"* which roll about the floor obeying commands from the microcomputer.
- Interfaces for *foreign printers, card readers,* etcetera.
- *Modems,* which connect the micro to mainframes or to distant data banks.
- *Networking systems* for downloading programs from one computer to other attached microcomputers.
- *Networking systems* for attaching one disk drive to many microcomputers (three to forty).

- *Networking systems* by which a master microcomputer controls the activities at twenty or thirty other microcomputers.
- *Networking systems* allowing one printer to be shared by many micros.
- *Networking systems* allowing one public TV monitor to be connected by switch to any micro in the room, and allowing users to see examples from selected micros elsewhere in the room.
- *Networking systems* for clustering of micros or word processing machines.
- *Extra memory modules* for expanding the computer memory.
- *Plug-in cartridges*, which provide instant programs related to subject matter or drill.

Money Option 25

Assist Laboratories and Scientists

Laboratories use microcomputers to control lasers, furnaces, steam pressures, and chemical flow rates; to measure acid levels; and so forth. Scientists may not care to master the technical trivia of connections to the microcomputer. They may prefer to hire a hardware expert to get a project working, then turn it over to the local staff.

Some of the requirements of laboratories are:

- Collecting sensory data from various sensing devices.
- Converting analog signals to digital signals, as when the computer must check the color of human blood in test tubes and assign a scaled number.
- Attaching plotters, printers, and other automatic timed reporting devices.
- Designing battery backup systems for microcomputers, disk drives, and printers.
- Maintaining a variety of clocks that can coordinate events.
- Managing microwave counters, Geiger counters, frequency counters, and mechanical counters.
- Timing precisely photographic or chemical events.
- Measuring the degree of acidity or alkalinity.
- Monitoring arrays of thermometers, pressure gauges, etcetera.

These types of hardware add-on options must be designed by someone, and most of us are not competent to do it. Therefore, those who can design circuits or who can promise that this circuit added to that microcomputer will produce desired results should advertise their services and fees. I for one would be glad to pay.

Turning Your
Word Processor into Gold

**MONEY
OPTION** **26** Provide Instant
Word Processing Services

Almost all microcomputers have a word processing program that you can purchase for personal pleasure or profit. More than forty different packages are available for the Apple computer, and even the inexpensive VIC computer has a "VIC Type-writer®" program. If you do not yet have a word processing program for your computer, you should ask your local computer dealer for a list of the programs available for your particular machine. Some of them cost as little as $20, so if you wish to experiment to see if you find pleasue in this type of work, it is not too expensive to give it a try.

Professional word processing programs may cost from $100 to $400, but they also have more features. So, before you go too far, you might want to have your local computer dealer demonstrate various types of word processing systems. If you don't have a disk drive and a printer with your system, you must obtain them if you hope to make money from this option.

Money Option 26

Provide Instant Word Processing Services

There are hundreds of corporate and college administrators who call in secretaries on Saturday and Sunday to retype reports and letters because one line or one paragraph in the Friday afternoon version requires changes. These administrators include owners of small businesses, school principals and superintendents, college deans, lawyers, and doctors.

With your instant word processing services, you would type such reports into your system and save the document on disk for later reference. You would run off a copy of the report and return it to the administrator for editing. The administrator would pencil in changes and corrections, after which you would recall the document from disk and with a few simple commands make the corrections, inserting new words, deleting sentences, and adding paragraphs.

Making these changes takes only a few minutes compared to the traditional retyping of the entire document. After your changes are completed, you can read the document on your computer screen to check it for accuracy and then print it again on the computer printer.

Last-minute corrections and changes are not a problem when you have a word processing service available. Reassure your clients that you don't mind at all if they send the document back to you for a dozen revision cycles. With the computer there is no penalty, and the cost will probably be less than if they tried to retype the document three or four times.

Set an hourly or daily fee rate and try to make the comparison between their old type-and-retype method and your word processing method apparent. Some word processing systems allow the names of people from mailing lists to be inserted into form letters for personalized mailings. Other services from your word processing system may open entirely new alternatives to your clients, causing more business opportunities to come your way.

After you have become proficient with the commands that direct your word processing program, you should not overlook the market for training and instruction of new owners of micros. The use of a word processing system seems so simple after you have mastered it, but many people avoid the use of word processing for years simply because no one is available to show them how to use the commands.

Inform your local computer dealer that you have started an instant word processing service for local businesses or anyone else who needs rapid turnaround. He may be able to direct some clients to you and on occasion may ask you to demonstrate to prospective buyers the professional use of text editing, footnoting, indexing, tables of contents, underlining, bold printing, chapter segmentation, page numbering, spelling verification, and all of the other features of modern word processors.

Starting a Microcomputer Dealership: Action and Money

Ever dream of owning and operating your own store? Heavy capital is required for taking on a McDonald's® franchise or a Pizza Hut®, but much less is required for starting a microcomputer store or a software store.

I am acquainted with more than forty computer store owners. Some of them got into the microcomputer business not because they were data processing experts or computer experts, but because they had a choice between running a frozen custard stand, a shoe store, or a computer store, and they chose the computer store. They succeed because they are sharp businessmen and women.

Since 1981, the microcomputer retail business has been extremely dynamic, resulting in strong profits for most of the more than 2,400 store owners in the United States.

The reason why micros should continue to bring profits is seen in the following table. We know from extensive research how many dollars will be spent collectively for microcomputers between now and 1985. There is room for many more dealers in this market, and the dollar profits come directly from moving goods such as disk drives, printers, computers, software packages, books, manuals, joy sticks, cartridges, and TV monitors. The data below were collected from many public sources and are confirmed by several research agencies.

What the U.S. Public Will Pay for Micros (Not Peripherals)*

	1982	1983	1984	1985	Total
Home	$ 210	$ 295	$ 391	$ 475	$ 1,371
School	70	90	117	145	332
Small Business	900	1,250	1,930	2,700	6,780
Office	290	540	922	1,450	3,222
Scientific	430	592	837	1,020	2,879
Total	$1,900	$2,767	$4,197	$5,790	$14,584

*In millions of dollars

If we assume that most of the home sales (as opposed to business sales) will be handled by Sears, Gimbels, Macys' and other department stores, seven-eighths of the business still remains for store dealerships to ring up in sales to businesses, schools, and offices. There probably has never been such a dynamic product as the microcomputer. Vendors sometimes have difficulty keeping staff at their corporate headquarters because the opportunities at the dealership level are so attractive.

Money Option 27

Start a Computer Store

A friend of mine, Tim Wordsman, started his store in 1979 before the vendors had established firm rules about computer stores and their appearances. Tim still runs his microcomputer business out of his basement gameroom. He supports three commissioned salesmen and earns more than $90,000 per year selling microcomputers. His secret—major in one market and get smart about that market.

Tim's market is schools. He responds to nearly every school bid in his state and wins many of them. He collects software suitable for schools to use and knows how to demonstrate it in timely and efficient ways. His sales staff are all former school administrators or teachers. He provides training and set-up services and keeps spare machines on hand, providing replacement computers when maintenance is required on school systems.

Today you would probably not be able to start a business like that in your basement. The vendors send their district sales managers out to your location to see whether or not you qualify to become an Apple dealer, a Commodore dealer, an Atari dealer, and so on.

The computer manufacturer wants store owners who will move equipment aggressively. If you apply to become a dealer, you will be visited by a district sales manager to see whether or not you are cluttered with other merchandise responsibilities. What experience have you had in retail sales? Is your location going to create a poor image for the computer products? The visitor who judges your qualifications will be asking these questions.

To qualify for a microcomputer store dealership, you will probably be required to jump these hurdles:

1. You will have to place an equipment order ranging from $40,000 to $60,000. The computer company will expect additional orders to follow each month or quarter. The initial order represents five to ten computer systems of various types and models.
2. You will be required to send a staff member to a training school to learn hardware maintenance procedures. You

will probably pay $500 to $1,500 for this training plus travel and expenses. You will also order kits of spare parts costing between $2,000 and $6,000.

3. You will be expected to display working models of microcomputers in your store showroom and to represent the vendor's products in a positive and knowledgeable way. You will be expected to have a display room, display stands, and all of the normal equipment required to operate a business. Incorporation papers and accounting standards must be in place.

4. You will be expected to order a minimal amount of the vendor's literature, software, and other products.

5. You will be expected to respond to public computer bids and other requests for price quotations. If you are not willing to give time to this aspect of the work, the vendor will not believe that you are serious and may doubt whether you will move very much hardware. Your aggressiveness in responding to all retail opportunities is a primary trait that will qualify or disqualify you as a potential dealer.

6. You will be expected to advertise in the newspapers and on the radio. Most vendors have a reimbursement or cooperative advertising arrangement that produces a twenty-five to thirty-five percent credit to you for all advertising costs. Some manufacturers require advance approval on local advertising so as to avoid investing in foolish and ineffective ads. This advertising reimbursement typically includes local television spots, movie ads, and catalog and magazine ads.

7. You will be expected to provide monthly and quarterly sales statistics and sales projections. The vendors desperately want to know what you can do for them next month and next quarter. "What can you do for me today?" is the slogan of many of the microcomputer companies.

8. You will be expected to learn how to operate and demonstrate software packages such as word processing, accounts receivable, Dow Jones Portfolio Management®, and educational programs. Training classes are provided by most manufacturers to teach you how to use these sys-

tems, and if you cannot attend you will be expected to send other store employees who will be demonstrating software to the public.

9. You will probably want to order several thousand dollars worth of software packages to display and sell in your store. Many of the software companies from whom you will purchase the programs are listed in Appendix H. If you write to these companies they may provide demonstration disks at very low cost, provided you seem likely to promote their software products.

After entering into this jungle of responsibilities, you will be rewarded with profits that get larger as you move more equipment. Sometimes new dealers who have not yet proven what

they can do for the microcomputer vendor are forced to operate under another dealer, which reduces the profit margin to as low as seventeen percent. Once you demonstrate that you can move equipment, your profit margin will vary typically from twenty-eight to forty percent, with higher sales bringing higher margins. These margins vary from vendor to vendor, but they are fairly well known and established.

Thus, on the sale of a $3,000 system with disk and printer, your thirty-two percent margin would bring $960 profit if you didn't give any discounts to the buyer. Out of this profit you would pay store rent, heat, light, sales commissions, two-thirds of your advertising, and other costs of sale. Whatever remained would go to salaries and profit. As you can see, retail sales require shrewd planning and thoughtful use of resources.

Money Option 28

Start a Software Store

Software stores operate quite differently from the computer hardware stores because they must attract people to come in from the street who may never have been a customer before.

In your software store, you must be able to demonstrate software packages reliably, efficiently, and on a variety of computers. Software for IBM micros, Osborne®, Victor®, and other evolving small business systems will fill the software stores with new products during the next two years.

Franchises for software stores became available in the spring of 1982. There are tremendous opportunities for demonstrating to the public the differences between software packages. Small business owners (lawyers or dentists, for example) cannot possibly sort out the attributes of each package that might serve their needs. They will therefore rely on the wisdom of the software expert at the software store, hoping that your advice can lead to the reliable and speedy startup of their new business system.

Someday there will be software dispensers standing beside candy and ice cream machines in airports and grocery stores. These machines will have slots for dollars instead of quarters, and will let you select software for between twenty and thirty varieties of computers. Vending machines will be set up for impulse software buying in such places as drug stores and grocery stores. Until then, software stores will continue to provide a much-needed advisory and consulting service.

If you have the skills and capital to undertake starting a store venture, why not pick out one of the software franchise distribution companies listed in the popular computer magazines? The software business requires less capital than a hardware store and it will probably become a dynamic market second only to the hardware at the computer store down the street.

Where will you get the software? How will you fill your display racks? Appendix H lists selected software companies that can supply dealers with prepackaged software. These suppliers commonly have a dealer's arrangement giving you a one-third to one-half price markup. In other words, what you buy for $10 you sell to the public for $18 to $20. That means that there are bigger percentage profits per item in the sale of software than in the sale of hardware. But you must sell quite a few programs to earn $1,000. Software stores *are* succeeding, and the market is waiting to be tapped.

10

Writing Articles and Books for Microcomputer Users

About seventy-five magazines are trying to find articles for their magazines each month on subjects that relate to microcomputers. Where do these 750 articles come from each month? People like you write about their experiences with microcomputers and express their opinions about the state of the art.

Besides the computer magazines, about 150 other magazines and journals not related to computers would like to publish microcomputer-related articles—maybe one or two articles each month in each of them—but they often can't find enough articles to meet the demand.

If we can store the world's knowledge on video disks, computer disks, microfilm, and movie film, you might think that the need for old-fashioned articles, manuals, and books would diminish. Not so.

A booklet of instructions could (or should) accompany every computer program written for every variety of microcomputer. That alone guarantees a continuing demand for writers and publishers.

Further, several hundred magazines want to publish articles describing user experiences with various computer programs, or how a school or company got organized to take advantage of a new program. They want to publish articles about how a program works, how dealers like selling it, how authors conceived the program, how the program compares with other competitive programs, or how the program could be used by gas station proprietors, stamp collectors, and Rotary clubs.

Many people assume that microcomputer articles should only be written by those who are technically competent or who have had many years of experience. This also is not true. I have read dozens of articles that almost anyone with writing skills could have written, carrying titles like these:

- "My First Twelve Hours with a Microcomputer"
- "Thoughts Upon Opening a Microcomputer Box"
- "My First Visit to a Computer Store"
- "How to Receive a Microcomputer Demonstration"
- "The Ten-Day Diary of a First-Time User"
- "A Beginner's Survey of a Microcomputer Keyboard"
- "A Tour of a Microcomputer Manual"
- "My First Experience Writing a BASIC Program"
- "Thoughts on Loading a Program from Tape"
- "Wiring Your Room for Your New Micro"
- "How to Care for Floppy Disks"
- "Buying a Computer for the Neighborhood—How to Share It"

Money Option 29

Write Articles for the Journals

Magazines pay between $100 and $300 for the articles they accept. Some authors call or write to the editors of various journals, explaining what type of article they are about to write. The editor may tell you that the journal has just purchased an article like the one you describe, thus saving you the trouble of writing it. Or, the editor may tell you that your idea is good, but "Could you slant it toward the experienced user, or toward the small business user, etc.?"

After you have published a few articles, your contacts at the publisher's headquarters should lead you to other writing opportunities. If your articles carry some substance, you will be asked to speak at various conferences and clubs.

You can approach your subject from any one of four directions. Each of these angles can form the basis for an article even if the subject remains the same. Suppose that you want to write about a new program that checks the spelling of words in word processing files. To that one subject you could apply the following four guides, resulting in four very different articles.

1. *Technical explanations.* In these articles you explain the technical aspects of your subject. Various themes could expand on the computer language used, the subroutines used, the hardware required, the organization of the program, the command structure, the protection methods, or the restart options.

2. *Application descriptions.* In these articles you describe the services performed by the application program. For example, you may describe how this program enables the user to dial into distant word processing files to check the spelling of words. Descriptions might include how to dial in, how to retrieve foreign files, how to store them on your local disk drive, how to compare two word processing files for differences, how to print personal lists of misspelled words, and how to obtain other related services.

3. *Human experiences.* These articles will present the story

of one, two, or three experiences related to microcomputers that people claim to have actually happened. The narrative will be full of short quotations from the people involved; descriptions of the interviews; and comments about their feelings, moods, fears, pleasures, successes, and failures. Human interest articles are quite popular. Photographs and drawings add interest and should be included. The brief article on page 109 by Roy Blount, Jr., illustrates this style of writing as it was read by thousands of TWA travellers in June, 1982.

4. *Administrative Viewpoints.* These articles will explain how to plan for new hardware or software, how to budget for it, how to organize or reorganize, how to finance a project, how to evaluate results, how to sell new ideas to people, how to enlist support, how to deal with problems, how to publicize, how to train users, how to create master plans, how to sustain Board or Trustee support, how to hire staff, how to retain staff, and so on.

Nearly all types of magazines are interested in microcomputer articles. The four types of articles listed could be written in popular style with plenty of "I" and "you" words scattered throughout, or they could be written more formally with no personal pronouns at all.

Also, specialty journals for hobbyists in such fields as stamp collecting, heavy horses, antique cars, or baroque music are all anxious to publish the ways in which micros are useful within each specialty area. This is especially true for the academic disciplines from colonial history to health and nursing occupations. Whatever your hobby area or interest, try writing an article about your use of mailing lists on a microcomputer, or data base filing systems as they apply to your hobby or discipline.

The demand for articles is so great that some people abandon the writing of software and begin to write articles or books full time.

APPLES AND ORANGES

By Roy Blount, Jr.

Roy Blount, Jr., lives in Mill River, Massachusetts, where an elderly manual typewriter is his constant companion.

Telling the computer what my first name was. That was my mistake. I have been married only twice, both times to women who called me by my first name. When a machine says to me something like "GOOD, ROY! YOU FOUND IT QUICKLY!" ("IT" being the "RETURN" key), I feel patronized. But also...engaged.

TWA Ambassador offered to place an Apple II in my home for a week or so. I thought, well sure. I had always wanted to give a computer a piece of my mind.

But I was put on the defensive as soon as I opened the big box the Apple was delivered in. I found some smaller boxes and a sheet of instructions, which advised me to be careful in opening the smaller boxes: "Those staples bite!"

Now, I have been bitten by staples many a time. But that is my lookout. If this carton of not-even-assembled-yet stuff had decided *after getting to know me better* that I deserved to be addressed as if I were its kindergarten pupil, well, all right, maybe.

As it happened, I had already been bitten, by the staples in that first big box. When Eve got into the apple, I suppose it said, "Those snakes lie." Great, now you tell me. "Those staples bite!" indeed! Also, that was the only part of the instructions I could understand. I withdrew from the carton with dignity.

Within 24 hours my fifteen-year-old daughter Ennis had assembled the Apple II in her bedroom, had hooked it up to her portable TV, and had figured out how to destroy the entire advancing horde of hideous aliens in the Stellar Invaders game without being wiped out herself. And my thirteen-year-old son Kirven had given the Apple Adventure game a ribald instruction. The machine's response, which offended both children's sense of delicacy, was "YOUR PLACE OR MINE?"

That same question, preceded by "IS THIS," was one I might well have addressed to the Apple. The Apple loomed large in my home. It had got my children to talking in terms of dwarves, RF Modulators, cursors and diskettes. Its beeps were more pervasive than the sounds of the heating system. Friends and neighbors would come to our door, walk right past me, and go upstairs to visit the computer.

It was time for me to take the Apple in hand. I went upstairs and yelled at it. It didn't respond. Then, somehow, there crept into my consciousness a little electronic-sounding wheedle: "WHATEVER YOU DO, PLEASE DON'T THROW ME INTO THE BRIARPATCH. THAT IS, PLEASE DON'T INSERT THE DISKETTE LABELED 'APPLE PRESENTS...APPLE' INTO MY DISK DRIVE AND START LEARNING HOW TO GIVE ME COMMANDS."

So I did. And it wasn't long before the machine had discovered my first name, and was using it to give *me* commands. And when I had proved to the Apple my ability to type out "YES," or something along those lines, it would ask me, "ISN'T THAT NEAT?"

I refused to answer such a question. But the Apple didn't acknowledge my refusal. And when I tried to get down to brass tacks by asking, "IF APPLE > THE BLOUNTS THEN PROVE IT," it responded by saying "SYNTAX ERROR."

That got my back up. Syntax is my bread and butter. As I say, however, I felt...engaged. I gritted my teeth and inserted the APPLE WRITER system diskette. I chose that diskette because I had always been afraid that some day a distinguished periodical would call me up and say, "We'd like to send you out to cover Armageddon on a fat expense account. Of course you'll have to file your copy on an Electronic Word Gizmo."

After a couple of hours with the APPLE WRITER, I felt prepared for such an assignment. I was even able to delete not-quite-trenchant phrases from my copy and then, if I felt nostalgic for them, to retrieve them from the automatic "storage buffer." "Nice little gizmo here," I found myself thinking.

But then the Apple's storage buffer gave me a serious turn. I was composing merrily, humming the old Apple right along, pretending I was covering the 1984 Big Brother Nominating Convention. I hit the retrieval key by mistake, and the following word marched resolutely into my text: "BLAGNONY."

I hadn't stored any "BLAGNONY" in the buffer. I didn't even know what it meant. But it looked insulting. This machine was not content to snipe at my syntax. It was now slinging an obscure, Hungarian-sounding epithet at, *and into*, my reportage.

But I'll tell you what I did. I didn't explode. I sat there for a few minutes and used the old bean. And this is what I realized: "BLAGNONY" was the sum of a series of individual typos that I had deleted and that the buffer had mindlessly (to my way of thinking) stored.

"You know what, Apple?" I crowed (orally). "You aren't telling me anything! You are a lower form of life than I am! You just sit there, like a clam, responding to stimuli! And even a clam would know better than 'B...L...A...G...N...O...N...Y' in, 'BLAGNONY' out!"

I went back through the "APPLE PRESENTS...APPLE" program. And this time I lied. I told the Apple my name was Norton. The Apple would tell me things like "YOU'RE MAKING GREAT PROGRESS, NORTON!" "And you're a neat little machine, Kumquat," I would chuckle (orally). I felt retrieved. ■

Money Option 30

Write Books About Microcomputers

Although there are more than 1,000 published books on the BASIC language, I know three people who are now under contract to write books on BASIC. They are writing these books for new micros that have just been introduced, or for publishers who need a new book for a certain audience.

There are probably dozens of BASIC books under contract to be written right now, and that is just one language out of many others that also have continuing needs for documentation or fresh presentations.

But it's not just the languages that require books. Books are also needed to describe each machine, each computer chip, each application area, each discipline's use of micros, each major software package, and so forth. For example, the manual that accompanies each microcomputer or each software package is rarely the final or best presentation of that product. Users who become acquainted with the product are eventually better equipped to write fresh and innovative views of the products, and there is good royalty income from writing such books.

That makes this money option a very real one. If you can step back from your preoccupation with the microcomputer itself and reflect on the perspective you have developed over a period of time, you may be able to form the outline of a book.

Don't write the book until you draft a rather full outline, after which you should mail it to the computer editor (or agent) for any of the publishers listed in the back of this book. If the publisher likes your idea, you will receive a contract which typically offers a royalty advance of $1,000 to $3,000. Be sure you don't underestimate the scope of the writing task, however. Even a 200-page book may require months of material collection, writing, editing, and selection of photographs. Once done, however, you will be pleased with the continuing income from royalties. If you have never written before, try articles before you attempt a book so that your writing skills can be developed adequately.

The satisfaction of book publication usually entices authors to write more books. The first book is the hardest, but the rewards are significant. After your title is listed in *Books in Print* and your name is placed on the card catalogs of libraries around the world, wholly new contacts and opportunities will open to you. As money options go, if you don't publish software, then magazine articles and books will generate about the best return on investment.

One final mandate. If you want to earn money as a writer, learn to use your word processing system to advantage. The inefficiency of typing and retyping manuscripts—even ten-page magazine articles—is simply unnecessary. If you want to write about microcomputers, learn how to use them. Your writings will carry more authenticity and credibility, and your output will triple. This book was written and edited on a CBM 8032 microcomputer using the Wordcraft® word processing system.

A literary agent should present most manuscripts to publishers, but since the demand for microcomputer books is so dynamic, many of the publishers in Appendix G may be willing to talk to you directly. Your contact at each publishing company will be with the computer science editor or the microcomputer editor.

My manuscript for the book *Future Mind: The Microcomputer New Medium, New Mental Environment* required two years of writing and editing before it was ready for publication. The entire manuscript of 450 pages was carried in a word processing system. Without the editing power of the word processor, the manuscript would have been virtually unmanageable. *Future Mind* applies the theories of Marshall McLuhan to the microcomputer scene, giving a new perspective for judging the effects of the micro on mind and culture. It is available from Little, Brown and Company, 34 Beacon Street, Boston, MA 02106.

11

Where Have All the Micros Gone? or Two Million Lost Money Machines

Here's a question to ponder. Where have all the computers gone?

There are more than thirty-eight million microcomputers in the world today. We know that because the factories have shipped that many microcomputer chips from their factories. Most of these miniature computer chips, however, have been hidden away in places where they slave behind the scenes performing a variety of automatic services.

You can't make money very easily from these hidden computers, however. They are locked into whatever they were preset to do. Pocket calculators contain them. So do some car dashboards and gasoline carburetors. Music synthesizers, telephone switchboards, giant computers, and photograph labs all contain these "locked-in" computers. They are really not available for people to use in their homes or on their desks.

About five million microcomputers remain, however, that have made entrance into our living rooms, homes, and offices. Three million of these computers are probably locked into TV game boxes, games such as "Simon Says®," or other hand-held, battery-powered games.

You will have difficulty making money from these game computers for the same reason—they are preprogrammed to do what they do, and consequently they don't give you flexible services to barter for money. Our family purchased a four-game black computer box that plays tennis, ping pong, hockey, and jai alai. It attaches to the TV set, and cost about $18.95 at a drug store. It isn't used very often, although it still operates perfectly.

Let's face it, we're not likely to produce any income from that computer.

Two million desktop microcomputers remain from which money *can* be earned. This book suggests that the desktop computers in homes, schools, and offices are potential money-makers. The best news is that technical programming skills are not required to obtain this income. In fact, many scientists and engineers do not realize income from their microcomputers despite their technical qualifications. Technical competence can be a great asset, but it is not required in many of the money-making options that have been presented.

Desktop microcomputers must meet several basic criteria in order to earn money for you. They must have a typewriter keyboard, a screen or television monitor, a microprocessor inside the machine, and BASIC language for writing or running programs.

These computers are commonly sold by about 3,000 stores throughout the country. Computerland stores and Radio Shack stores are typical of the dealers who market and sell desktop micros. A few large mail-order houses began to sell microcomputers by mail in 1981. Fisher Scientific and UARCO are examples of mail-order sources.

Many department stores are beginning to sell desktop microcomputers, and in 1985 mass merchandising will probably supply more than 900,000 desktop computers *each year* to the general public. More microcomputers are predicted to be sold in 1985 than were sold from 1977 to 1981 combined. Why? Because prices are dropping and the features on the machines are constantly improving.

In 1977, Commodore's PET was the first micro to be priced under $800. In 1982, the Timex-Sinclair 1000 was priced at $99. The miniature keyboard on the Timex is a flat plastic panel, but all the features of a true computer are built into it. When department stores and drug stores provide several models and makes of low-priced micros to the public, we will surely become a more computer-literate society.

What does this do to us? Where is it taking us? During the next few years, millions of people will pass through a period of experimentation and learning. Software for the rapidly evolving machines will be written, sold, used, and abandoned as newer microcomputers and more pleasing software become available.

The absence of standards among machines guarantees very rapid evolution. Wave after wave of uninitiated users will seek understanding and training. Many who can't afford the typical $1,000 to $4,000 fee (for a complete system with disk and printer in 1983) will wish to rent one in order to avoid the twelve-month obsolescence cycles of the rapidly changing models. They will be willing to pay to learn about the equipment and will pay for training if it helps to get them onto the computer bandwagon.

No occupational group is immune from the appeal and the services offered by these microcomputers. The availability of very low-cost hardware points sooner or later toward every lawyer, accountant, flower shop, rock band, gas station, hardware store, and art shop using computers as a means of reducing operating costs and managing the business more cost effectively. Students will use them and so will teachers, corporate executives and shop mechanics, clergymen and salesmen.

It is our transition from a machine-based society to an electronic-based society, from a product-based economy to an information-based economy that will generate and enlarge the money-making opportunities described in this book.

The number of people who had or will have access to computers varies wildly from year to year—but the number always goes up. Between 1954 and 1964, when computers typically cost three million dollars, there may have been 100,000 people in the United States who had access to computers. Between 1964 and 1974, when the average computer cost about one million dollars, there may have been 800,000 people in the workforce associated with these machines.

Hobbyists began to buy $8,000 microcomputer systems between 1974 and 1977, enlarging the number of people who could experience and understand the opportunities associated with small computers. Then, with the introduction of microcomputers under $1,000 in 1977, the in-group swelled to approximately two million people by 1980. Most of these people worked with computers in ways that forced them to write software programs or else to use business programs written by others.

Then, a startling phenomenon could be seen. In about 1979 department stores and computer stores began to sell video games ($400 microcomputers), which would perform a limited portion of the larger services that could be obtained from the $900 computers. Flashy (and noisy) display areas were erected in the electronics sections of many department stores. Children and young adults crowded around these displays, wielding joy sticks, pushing buttons, and steering space ships across the screens.

Today the arcades at the malls and shopping centers further prepare the culture for the acceptance of computer-assisted everything. Walking among the players in the arcades today, listening to the sights and sounds of the computer-assisted games, you will find some players who regularly drop as much as $40 or more into the coin slots each month. With that much money being spent, maybe you should be renting your desktop computer to these players. It might be cheaper for them. Many of the arcade games are available on the desktop microcomputers. Even though you might not be attracted to the games and space battles yourself, thousands of other people are hooked on these games. You can talk to them in the game rooms at motels and malls.

There are about 240 million people in the United States. Our resistance to the idea of using microcomputers has been lowered by the relentless services of microcomputers. They come toward us from every direction. The public glimpses microcomputers at the bank, in toys at the toy store, in color displays on the boardwalk, in the arcades, and in home television games purchased as Christmas gifts. Children tell about using microcomputers at school. Teachers tell about children who have microcomputers at home. Television programs award computers as gifts.

Therefore, the two million people (or offices) who possess desktop microcomputers today have something that 238 million other people will want to learn about between 1983 and 1988. If 200,000 computer owners decide to try one or more of the money-making options in this book, that creates a makeshift ratio of 1,000 to 1, comparing those who could provide services with the others who probably want services.

Where have all the computers gone? No one knows for sure. Many people don't even send in the warranty card when they buy a microcomputer, especially if they paid less than $500 for it. Thousands of micros have gone into closets to gather dust. This book encourages you to dust them off and (at least) donate them to a school or church. Better yet, if you learn how to use them, you will have significant opportunities to sell services as a teacher, tutor, or software writer.

Appendices

Appendix A

Selected Microcomputer Journals and Newsletters

AEDS Monitor
Association of Educational
  Data Systems
1201 16th Street NW
Washington, DC 20036

Apple Education News
10260 Bandley Drive
Cupertino, CA 95014

Byte
Box 981
Farmingdale, NY 11737

Classroom Computer News
Intentional Educations, Inc.
51 Spring Street
Watertown, MA 02172

Commodore Magazine
487 Devon Park Drive
Wayne, PA 19087

Compute
Small System Services, Inc.
P.O. Box 5406
Greensboro, NC 27403

Computer
10662 Los Vaqueros Circle
Los Alamitos, CA 90720

Computer Business News
375 Cochituate Road
Framingham, MA 01701

Computer Merchandising
15720 Ventura Boulevard
  #610
Encino, CA 91436

Computer Products
20 Community Place
Morristown, NJ 07960

Computer Systems News
333 East Shore Road
Manhasset, NY 11030

Computer Town USA
P.O. Box E
Menlo Park, CA 94025

Computers and People
Berkeley Enterprises
815 Washington Street
Newtonville, MA 02160

Computerworld
375 Cochituate Road
Framingham, MA 01701

Computer Retailing
1760 Peachtree Road NW
Atlanta, GA 30357

Computer Graphics World
54 Mint Street
San Francisco, CA 94108

Computer-Using Educators
CUE, Inc.
Alhambra High School
150 E Street
Martinez, CA 94553

Computing Teacher
University of Oregon
Eugene, OR 97403

Conduit Pipeline
P.O. Box 388
Iowa City, IA 52244

Creative Computing
P.O. Box 789-M
Morristown, NJ 07960

Cursor
The Code Works
Box 550
Goleta, CA 93017

Educators Handbook and Software Directory
Vital Information, Inc.
7899 Mastin Drive
Overland Park, KS 66204

Educational Computer Magazine
10439 North Stelling Road
Cupertino, CA 95014

Edunet News
Educom
P.O. Box 364
Princeton, NJ 08540

Electronic Education
Electronic Communications, Inc.
Suite 220
1311 Executive Center Drive
Tallahassee, FL 32301

Electronic Learning
Scholastic, Inc.
50 West 44th Street
New York, NY 10036

Electronic Playworld
504 Yonge Street
Toronto, Ontario M4Y1Y3
Canada

Electronic Products
645 Stewart Avenue
Garden City, NY 11530

Hands-On
Technical Education Research Centers
8 Elliot Street
Cambridge, MA 02138

IEEE Spectrum
345 East 47th Street
New York, NY 10017

Information and Records Management
250 Fulton Avenue
Hempstead, NY 11551

Information Systems News
333 East Shore Road
Manhasset, NY 11030

Interface Age
16704 Marquardt Avenue
Cerritos, CA 90701

Interactive Computing
Journal of the Association of Computer Users
P.O. Box 9003
Boulder, CO 80301

Jinsam Newsletter
Box 274
Riverdale, NY 10463

Kilobaud Microcomputing
80 Pine Street
Peterborough, NH 03485

Lawrence Hall of Science Newsletter
University of California
Centenial Drive
Berkeley, CA 94720

Leisure Time Electronics
124 East 40th Street
New York, NY 10016

MECC Newsletter
2520 Broadway Drive
Lauderdale, MN 55113

Micro—The 6502 Journal
Micro Ink, Inc.
34 Chelmsford Street
Chelmsford, MA 01824

Microphy's Programs
2048 Ford Street
Brooklyn, NY 11229

Microprocessor Newsletter
1210-A King Street
Wilmington, DE 19801

Micro-Scope
JEM Research Discovery Park
University of Victoria
P.O. Box 1700
Victoria, BC Canada V8W2Y2

Microsift
Northwest Regional Educational Laboratory
500 Lindsay Building
710 Southwest Second Avenue
Portland, OR 97204

Mini-Micro Computer Report
7620 Little River Turnpike
Annandale, VA 22003

Office Product News
645 Steart Avenue
Garden City, NY 11530

Pipeline Conduit
P.O. Box 388
Iowa City, IA 52244

Purser's Magazine
Box 466
El Dorado, CA 95623

School Courseware Journal
4919 N. Millbrook 222B
Fresno, CA 93726

School Microware
Dresden Association
P.O. Box 246
Dresden, ME 04342

Small Business Computers
33 Watchung Plaza
Montclair, NY 07042

Small Systems World
53 West Jackson Boulevard
Chicago, IL 60604

Softtalk
Softtalk Publishing, Inc.
10432 Burbank Boulevard
North Hollywood, CA 91601

Software
1 Tiger Plaza
Box 8359
Newport Beach, CA 92660

Software Digest
7620 Little River Turnpike
Annandale, VA 22003

Software News
5 Kane Industrial Drive
Hudson, MA 01749

The Source Magazine
1616 Anderson Road
McLean, VA 22102

Technology Illustrated
P.O. Box 2804
Boulder, CO 80321

The Journal
Technological Horizons in Education
P.O. Box 992
Acton, MA 01720

80 Microcomputing for TRS-80 Users
P.O. Box 981
Farmingdale, NY 11737

Appendix B

Selected User Clubs and User Groups

California

Apple for the Teacher
Ted Perry
5848 Riddio Street
Citrus Heights, CA 95610

BAMBUG
1450 53rd Street
Emeryville, CA

Computer-Using Educators (CUE)
Independence High School
1776 Educational Park Drive
San Jose, CA 95133

Downey-Bellflower User Group
14944 Bayou Avenue
Bellflower, CA 90706

Lawrence Hall of Science
Centenial Drive
University of California—
Berkeley, Room 254
Berkeley, CA 94720

Lincoln Computer Club
750 East Yosemite
Manteca, CA 95336

North Orange County Computer Club
3030 Topaz, Apartment A
Fullerton, CA 92361

PALS Livermore Society
886 South K
Livermore, CA 94550

PET on the Air
525 Crestlake Drive
San Francisco, CA 94132

PUG of Silicon Valley
22355 Rancho Ventura
Cupertino, CA 95014

Sacramento PET
P.O. Box 28314
Sacramento, CA 95813

San Diego PUG
3562 Union Street
San Diego, CA 92109

SPINX
314 10th Street
Oakland, CA 94615

Valley Computer Club
2006 Magnolia Boulevard
Burbank, CA 91505

Walnut Creek PET Users Club
1815 Ygnacio Valley Road
Walnut Creek, CA 94596

Florida

Jacksonville Area PET Society
401 Monument Road, #177
Jacksonville, FL 32211

South Florida PET Users Group
7170 Southwest 11th Street
West Hollywood, FL 33023

Illinois

Central Illinois PET Owners
2730 Townway Road, #E-54
Danville, IL 61832

PET VIC Club
40 South Lincoln
Mundelein, IL 60060

Indiana
PET Users
P.O. Box 36014
Indianapolis, IN 46236

Iowa
PET Users Group
1321 42nd Street
Cedar Rapids, IA 52403

Maryland
Association of Personal Computer Users
5014 Rodman Road
Bethesda, MD 20016

Massachusetts
EDUSIG
Digital Equipment Users
Group
One Iron Way
Marlboro, MA 01752
The Boston Computer Society
Three Center Plaza
Boston, MA 02108

Michigan
Michigan Association for Computer Users in Learning
33550 Van Born Road
Wayne, MI 48184
PET User Group
2235 Lakeshore Drive
Muskegon, MI 49441
Toledo PETS
734 Donna Drive
Temperance, MI 48182

Missouri
St. Louis Club
46 Westwood Court
St. Louis, MO 63131

Nevada
Las Vegas PET Users
4884 Iron Avenue
Las Vegas, NV 89110

New Hampshire
Northern New England Computer Society
P.O. Box 69
Verlin, NH 03570

New Jersey
Amateur Computer Group 18
Alpine Drive
Wayne, NJ 07470

Amateur Computer Group of New Jersey
UCTI 1776 Raritan Road
Scotch Plains, NJ 07076

Somerset Users Club
49 Marcy Street
Somerset, NJ 08873

New York

Long Island PET Society
Harborfields High School
Taylor Avenue
Greenlawn, NY 11740

Long Island VIC Enthusiasts
(LIVE)
17 Picadilly Road
Great Neck, NY 11023

PET User Club of Westchester
Box 1280
White Plains, NY 10602

Ohio

Dayton Area PET User Group
933 Livingston Drive
Xenia, OH 45385

Oregon

Northwest Council for Computers in Education
Eastern Oregon State College
La Grande, OR 97850

Northwest PET Users Group
2134 Northeast 45th Avenue
Portland, OR 97213

Pennsylvania

PACS PET Users Group
20th and Olnew Streets
Philadelphia, PA 19116

PET User Group
P.O. Box 371
Montgomeryville, PA 18936

Tennessee

Society of Data Educators
983 Fairmeadow Road
Memphis, TN 38117

Texas

PET User Group
Texas A and M University
College Station, TX 77843

PET Users
2001 Bryan Towers 3800
Dallas, TX 75201

SCOPE
1020 Summit Circle
Carrolton, TX 75006

Texas Computer Education Association
7131 Midbury
Dallas, TX 75230

Utah

Utah PUG
2236 Washington Boulevard
Ogden, UT 84401

Virginia

Northern Virginia PET Users
2045 Eakins Court
Reston, VA 22091

Washington

Northwest PET User Group
Box 482
Vashon, WA 98070

Wisconsin

Sewpus
P.O. Box 21851
Milwaukee, WI 53221

Appendix C

Selected Microcomputer Manufacturers

Alpha Microsystems
17881 Sky Park North
Irvine, CA 92713

Altos Computer Systems
2360 Bering Drive
San Jose, CA 95101

APF Electronics, Inc.
1501 Broadway
New York, NY 10036

Apple Computer, Inc.
10260 Bandley Drive
Cupertino, CA 95014

Applied Digital Systems, Inc.
100 Marcus Boulevard
Hauppauge, NY 11788

Associated Computer Industries
17751 H Sky Park East
Irvine, CA 92714

Atari, Inc.
1265 Borregas Avenue
Sunnyvale, CA 94086

Bell & Howell
7100 McCormick Road
Chicago, IL 60645

CADO System Corp.
2771 Toledo Street
Torrance, CA 90503

Campbell Scientific, Inc.
815 West 1800 North
Box 551
Logan, UT 84321

Canon USA, Inc.
Systems Division
One Canon Plaza
Lake Success, NY 11040

Casio, Inc.
15 Gardner Road
Fairfield, NJ 07006

Commodore Business Machines
487 Devon Park Drive
Wayne, PA 19087

Commodore Canada
3370 Pharmacy Avenue
Agincourt, Ontario M1W 2K4
Canada

Compal, Inc.
6300 Variel Avenue
Woodland Hills, CA 91367

Computhink
965 West Maude Avenue
Sunnyvale, CA 94086

Control Data Corporation
8100 34th Avenue South
Minneapolis, MN 55440

CPT Corporation
8100 Mitchell Road
Minneapolis, MN 55440

Cromemco, Inc.
2800 Bernardo Avenue
Mountain View, CA 94043

Cyberdata
2611 Garden Road
Monterey, CA 93940

Datamac Computer Systems
680 Almanor Avenue
Sunnyvale, CA 94086

Datapoint Corporation
9725 Datapoint Drive
San Antonio, TX 78284

Delta Products
15392 Assembly Lane
Huntington Beach, CA 92649

Digilog Business Systems, Inc.
Park Drive and Welsh Road
Montgomeryville, PA 18936

Digital Equipment Corporation
One Iron Way
Marboro, MA 01752

Digital Microsystems
1840 Embarcadenno
Oakland, CA 94611

Digital Scientific Corporation
11425 Sorrento Valley Road
San Diego, CA 92121

Durango Systems, Inc.
3003 N. First Street
San Jose, CA 95134

Dynabyte
115 Independence Drive
Menlo Park, CA 94025

Exidy
1234 Elk Drive
Sunnyvale, CA 94086

Fujitsu
2985 Kiefer
Santa Clara, CA 95051

Gimix, Inc.
1337 West 37th Place
Chicago, IL 60609

Heath Company
Benton Harbor, MI 49022

Hewlett-Packard
1000 Northeast Circle
  Boulevard
Corvallis, OR 97330

Hitachi Sales Corporation of America
401 West Artesia Boulevard
Compton, CA 90220

IMS International
2800 Lockheed Way
Carson City, NV 89701

Industrial Micro Systems
628 North Eckhoff Street
Orange, CA 92668

Intel Corporation
3065 Bowers Avenue
Santa Clara, CA 95051

Intelligent Systems
225 Technology Parkway
Norcross, GA 30092

International Business Machines Corporation
Box 1328
Boca Raton, FL 33432

Intertec Data Systems Corporation
2300 Broad River Road
Columbia, SC 29210

Ithaca Intersystems, Inc.
1650 Hanshaw Road
Ithaca, NY 14850

Lexor Corporation
7100 Hayvenhurst
Van Nuys, CA 91406

Logical Business Machines
1294 Hammerwood Avenue
Sunnyvale, CA 94086

Micro Computer Technology, Inc.
3304 West MacArthur
  Boulevard
Santa Ana, CA 92704

Micro Five Corporation
17791 Sky Park Circle
Irvine, CA 92714

Micro Technology Unlimited
2806 Hillsborough Street
Raleigh, NC 27605

MicroDaSys, Inc.
2811 Wilshire Boulevard
Santa Monica, CA 90403

**Midwest Scientific In-
   struments, Inc.**
220 West Cedar
Olathe, KS 66061

Monroe Systems for Business
The American Road
Morris Plains, NJ 07950

**National Semiconductor Cor-
   poration**
2900 Semiconductor Drive
Santa Clara, CA 95051

NEC Home Electronics USA
1401 Estes Avenue
Elk Grove Village, IL 60007

Nestar
2585 East Bayshore Road
Palo Alto, CA 94303

NNC Electronics
15631 Computer Lane
Huntington Beach, CA 92649

NorthStar Computers, Inc.
14440 Catalina Street
San Leandro, CA 94577

Novell Data Systems, Inc.
1170 North Industrial Park
   Drive
Orem, UT 84057

Ohio Scientific, Inc.
1333 South Chillicothe Road
Aurora, OH 44202

Onyx Systems
73 East Trimble Road
San Jose, CA 95131

Osborne Computer
26500 Corporate Avenue
Hayward, CA 94545

Panasonic
One Panasonic Way
Secaucus, NJ 07094

Pertec Computer Corporation
12910 Culver Boulevard
Los Angeles, CA 90009

Polymorphic Systems
460 Ward Drive
Santa Barbara, CA 93111

Prodigy Systems, Inc.
497 Lincoln Highway
Iselin, NJ 08830

**Qantel/Mohawk Data
   Sciences**
4142 Point Eden Way
Hayward, CA 94545

Quasar Company
9401 West Grand Avenue
Franklin Park, IL 60131

Quay Corporation
527 Industrial Way West
Eatontown, NJ 07724

Radio Shack
1400 One Tandy Center
Fort Worth, TX 76102

Ramtek
2211 Lawson Lane
Santa Clara, CA 95050

RCA Microcomputer Marketing
New Holland Avenue
Lancaster, PA 17604

Rockwell International
Microelectronics Division
Box 3669
Anaheim, CA 92803

Scientific Data Systems
344 Main Street
Venice, CA 90291

Sentinel Computer Corporation
9902 Carver Road
Cincinnati, OH 45242

Sharp Electronics
10 Sharp Plaza
Paramus, NJ 07652

Smoke Signal Broadcasting
31336 Via Colinas
Westlake Village, CA 91361

Southwest Technical Products Corporation
219 West Rhapsody
San Antonio, TX 78216

STC Systems
Nine Brook Avenue
Maywood, NJ 07607

Symco Systems, Inc.
7182 North Park Drive
Pennsauken, NJ 08109

Tarbell Electronics
950 Dovlen Place
Carson, CA 90746

Techtran Systems
200 Commerce Drive
Rochester, NY 14623

TEI Systems
5075 South Loop East
Houston, TX 77033

Telcon Industries, Inc.
1401 Northwest 69th Street
Fort Lauderdale, FL 33309

Televideo Systems, Inc.
1170 Morse Avenue
Sunnyvale, CA 94086

Terak Corporation
14151 North 76th Street
Scottsdale, AZ 85260

Texas Instruments, Inc.
Box 10508
Lubbock, TX 79408

Three Rivers Computer Corporation
160 North Craig Street
Pittsburgh, PA 15213

Timex-Sinclair
Timex Corporation
Waterbury, CT 06720

Toshiba Information Systems
2441 Michelle Drive
Tustin, CA 92680

Vector Graphic, Inc.
500 North Ventu Park Road
Thousand Oaks, CA 91320

Wang Laboratories, Inc.
One Industrial Avenue
Lowell, MA 01851

Western Digital Corporation
3128 Red Hill Avenue
Costa Mesa, CA 92626

Xerox Corporation
6416 Wrenwood
Dallas, TX 75252

Yang Electronic Systems
307 Compton Avenue
Laurel, MD 20810

Zenith Data Systems
1000 Milwaukee Avenue
Glenview, IL 60025

Zilog, Inc.
10460 Bubb Road
Cupertino, CA 95014

Appendix D

Selected Software Directories

Apple II Blue Book
WIDL Video Chicago
5245 West Diversey Avenue
Chicago, IL 60539

Apple II/III Software Directory
Vanloves Vital Information, Inc.
350 Union Station
Kansas City, MO 64108

Apple Educators Newsletter
9525 Lucern
Ventura, CA 93003

Appleseed
Software Publications
6 South Street
Milford, NH 03055

Commodore Software Encyclopedia
Commodore Business Machines
487 Devon Park Drive
Wayne, PA 19087

Datapro Directory of Microcomputer Software
1805 Underwood Boulevard
Delran, NJ 08075

Educational Computing Resources Directory
Classroom Computer News
51 Spring Street
Watertown, MA 02172

Educational Software Directory
Sterling Swift Publishing Company
P.O. Box 188
Manchaca, TX 78652

Educator's Handbook and Software Directory
Vital Information, Inc.
350 Union Station
Kansas City, MO 64108

Huntington Computing Catalog
P.O. Box 787
Corcoran, CA 93212

International Microcomputer Software Directory
Imprint Software
420 South Howes Street
Fort Collins, CO 80521

K-12 Micro Media
P.O. Box 17
Valley Cottage, NY 10989

March, Inc.
280 Linden Drive
Branford, CT 06082

Microcomputers Corporation Catalog
P.O. Box 191
Rye, NY 10580

Microcomputers in Education
Queve, Inc.
5 Chapel Hill Drive
Fairfield, CT 05432

Opportunities for Learning
Department L-4
8950 Lurline Avenue
Chatsworth, CA 91311

Queue
5 Chapel Hill Drive
Fairfield, CT 06432

**Radio Shack Application and
   Software Sourcebook**
Radio Shack
1600 One Tandy Center
Fort Worth, TX 76102

School Microware Directory
Dresden Associates
P.O. Box 246
Dresden, ME 04342

Skarbeks Software Directory
11990 Dorsett Road
St. Louis, MO 63043

Software Vendor Directory
Micro-Software Services, Inc.
P.O. Box 482
Nyack, NY 10960

Training's Yellow Pages
731 Hennepin Avenue
Minneapolis, MN 55403

TRS-80 Software Directory
Radio Shack
1600 One Tandy Center
Fort Worth, TX 76102

**Vanloves Apple II/III Soft-
   ware Directory**
Vital Information, Inc.
350 Union Station
Kansas City, MO 64108

Appendix E

Software Agents

The people listed here have extensive experience in the marketing of microcomputer software and in the sale of software through publishing companies and software houses.

The general reimbursement plan presented in Money Options 7 and 8 are familiar to these people. However, each of them operates independently; they will present their terms when you contact them.

Each person is known to this writer and is believed to be reliable and knowledgeable about the current state of the industry. Software authors should exercise judgment in their choice of agent and the terms of relationship, for which no guarantee is implied.

James Bussey
3824 Cougar Place
Modesto, CA 95356

Kristen Saunders Coombs
P.O. Box 201, SHS
Duxbury, MA 02332

Electronic Communications, Inc.
Suite 220
1311 Executive Center Drive
Tallahassee, FL 32301

Andrew T. Fowler
5229 Powhatan Avenue
Norfolk, VA 23508
(804) 440-3189

Dr. Lyndal Hutcherson
2800 Arcadia Street
Carrollton, TX 75007

Terrence M. Wright
Eagle Software
110 West Lancaster Avenue
Wayne, PA 19087

Appendix F

Workshop Resources

Computer Literary Show and Tell Kit

Sterling Swift Publishing Company
1600 Fortview Road
Austin, TX 78704

Priced at $89.95, this kit provides demonstration software and instructions for workshop leaders.

Curriculum Guide for Computer Literacy

HUMRO
300 North Washington Street
Alexandria, VA 22314

A grant from the National Science Foundation funded this research. The document surveys computer course objectives for kindergarten through eighth grade. It includes a librarian's guide for establishing a computer resource center, classroom activities, films, and teacher training materials.

Computer Literacy: An Introductory Course

Continental Press
Educational Publishers
Elizabethtown, PA 17022

This comprehensive curriculum was compiled by a working committee of teachers and computer leaders in Pennsylvania over a period of two years. The product includes student exercises, film, posters, software on disk or tape, and other materials which can be used with grades seven to adult.

Lias, Edward J. Future Mind: *The Microcomputer, New Medium, New Mental Environment*

Little, Brown and Company
34 Beacon Street
Boston, MA 02106

The theories of Marshal McLuhan are applied to the computer scene, evaluating its effects on life and culture. Provides backgrounds for the non-technical reader and gives predictions to the year 2040. Supplementary reading for computer literacy courses or workshops.

Luehrmann, Arthur and Herb Peckham. *Computer Literacy*

Computer Literacy Company
1466 Grizzly Peak Boulevard
Berkeley, CA 94708

Several major books, laboratory manuals, and other resources are available from the Computer Literacy Company. The materials are validated and widely used. Emphasis on structured programming.

Moursund, David. *School Administrators Introduction to Instructional Use of Computers*

International Council for Computers in Education
Eastern Oregon State College
La Grande, OR 97850

Surveys a variety of instructional uses that computers serve in schools. Lists resources, curricula, and objectives.

Rice, Jean M. *My Friend the Computer* and *Computers are Fun*

T. S. Denison and Company
9601 Newton Avenue South
Minneapolis, MN 55437

These books are used with grades five through adult as introductory guides. Teacher's manuals are also available.

Wall, Elizabeth S. *Children's Books for Computer Awareness*

Bayshoe Books
P.O. Box 848
Nokomis, FL 33555

An excellent list of about fifty books that can be used in children's workshops or courses.

Appendix G

Book Publishers Who Sell Microcomputer Software

Addison-Wesley Publishing
2725 Sand Hill Road
Menlo Park, CA 94025

Borg-Warner Educational Systems
600 West University Drive
Arlington Heights, IL 60004

Continental Press, Inc.
Educational Publishers
Elizabethtown, PA 17022

Educational Testing Service
Rosedale Road
Princeton, NJ 08541

Evans Newton, Inc.
447745 East Redfield Road
Scottsdale, AZ 85260

Follett Publishing Company
1010 West Washington
Boulevard
Chicago, IL 60607

Hayden Book Company
50 Essex Street
Rochelle Park, NJ 07662

Holt, Rinehart and Winston
383 Madison Avenue
New York, NY 10017

Houghton Mifflin Company
One Beacon Street
Boston, MA 02107

Howard W. Sams and Company
4300 West 62nd Street
Indianapolis, IN 46206

McGraw-Hill Book Company
1221 Avenue of the Americas
New York, NY 10020

Charles E. Merrill Publishing
1300 Alum Creek Drive
Columbus, OH 43216

Milliken Publishing
1100 Research Boulevard
St. Louis, MO 63132

Milton-Bradley Company
Shaker Road
East Longmeadow, MA 01028

Random House
201 East 50th Street
New York, NY 10022

Reader's Digest
Education Division
Pleasantville, NY 10022

Reston Publishing Company, Inc.
11480 Sunset Hills Road
Reston, VA 22090

Richard D. Irwin, Inc.
Homewood, IL 60430

Science Research Associates, Inc.
155 North Wacker Drive
Chicago, IL 60606

Scholastic Magazine, Inc.
50 West 44th Street
New York, NY 10036

Scott, Foresman and Com-
pany
1900 East Lake Avenue
Glenview, IL 60025

South Western Publishing
5101 Madison Road
Cincinnati, OH 45227

Sterling Swift Publishing
Company
1600 Fortview Road
Austin, TX 78704

Appendix H

Software Companies

AB Computers
252 Bethlehem Pike
Colmar, PA 18915

Abacus Software
P.O. Box 7211
Grand Rapids, MI 49510

Access
P.O. Box 8726
West Covina, CA 91790

Acorn Software Products, Inc.
634 North Carolina Avenue
   Southeast
Washington, DC 20003

Adventure Internol
Box 3435
Longwood, FL 32750

Alphanetics
P.O. Box 597
Forestville, CA 95436

Apple Puget Sound Program Library Exchange
304 Main Avenue South
Renton, WA 98055

Applications Research Company
13460 Robleda Road
Los Altos Hills, CA 94022

Applied Educational Systems
RFD #2, Box 213
Dunbarton, NH 03301

Big Five
P.O. Box 9078
Van Nuys, CA 91409

Bits & Bytes
33 Church Street
Fredonia, NY 14063

BPI Systems, Inc.
1600 West 38th #444
Austin, TX 78731

BrainBox
601 West 26th Street
New York, NY 10001

Briley Software
P.O. Box 2913
Livermore, CA 94550

Broderbund Software
2 Vista Wood Way
San Rafael, CA 94901

BT Enterprises
171 Hawkins Road
Centerreach, NY 11720

Business Enhancement
1711 East Valley Parkway
   #109
Escondido, CA 92027

Byte Me Computer Shoppe
327 Captain's Walk
New London, CT 06320

Canadian Micro Distributors, Ltd.
365 Main Street
Milton, Ontario L9T 1P7
Canada

CFI
875 West End Avenue
New York, NY 10025

CMS Software Systems, Inc.
5115 Menefee Drive
Dallas, TX 75227

The Code Works
P.O. Box 550
5778 Hollister
Goleta, CA 93017

Cognitive Products
330 Eastside Drive
Bloomington, IN 47401

Comaldor
P.O. Box 356 PS 0
Toronto, Ontario M4A 2N9
Canada

Comm Data Systems, Inc.
P.O. Box 325
Milford, MI 48042

Competitive Software
21650 Maple Glen Drive
Edwardsburg, MI 49112

Computer Curriculum Corp.
1070 Arastradero Road
Palo Alto, CA 94304

Computer House Division
1407 Clinton Road
Jacksonville, MI 49202

Computer Specialties, Inc.
701 East Lincoln Avenue
Melbourne, FL 32901

Computeronics, Inc.
50 North Pascack Road
Spring Valley, NY 10977

Conduit
P.O. Box 388
Iowa City, IA 52244

Connecticut Microcomputer
150 Pocono Road
Brookfield, CT 06804

Contract Services Association
706 South Euclid
Anaheim, CA 92802

Cooks Computer Company
1905 Bailey Drive
Marshalltown, IA 50185

Cow Bay Computing
P.O. Box 515
Manhasset, NY 11030

Creative Computing Software
Morris Plains, NJ 07950

Creative Software
P.O. Box 4030
Mountain View, CA 94040

Cyberia, Inc.
2330 Lincoln Way
Ames, IA 50010

Dakin5
7475 Dakin Street
Denver, CO 80221

Datamost
19273 Kenya Street
Northridge, CA 91326

Designware
185 Berry Street
San Francisco, CA 94107

Dynacomp, Inc.
1427 Monroe Avenue
Rochester, NY 14618

Eagle Software Publishing, Inc.
110 West Lancaster Avenue
Wayne, PA 19087

Ed-Sci Development
460 Beacon Street
San Francisco, CA 94131

Edu-Ware
22222 Sherman Way
Canoga Park, CA 91303

Evans Newton, Inc.
7335 East Acoma Drive
Scottsdale, AZ 85260

EXC Computer Company
267 North Main Street
Walnut Creek, CA 94596

Galactic Software, Ltd.
11520 North Washington Road
Mequon, WI 53092

Halpurr Software
24500 Glenwood Drive
Los Gatos, CA 95030

Hartley Courseware, Inc.
P.O. Box 431
Dimondale, MI 48821

Huntington Computing
P.O. Box 1235
Corcoran, CA 93212

Ideatech Company
P.O. Box 62451
Sunnyvale, CA 94088

IDSI Innovative Design Software, Inc.
P.O. Box 1658
Las Cruces, NM 88004

InfoDesigns, Inc.
6905 Telegraph Road
Birmingham, MI 48010

Instant Software, Inc.
Elm Street & Route One
Peterborough, NH 03458

Instructional Communications Technology, Inc.
10 Stepar Place
Huntington Station, NY 11746

Instructional Development Systems
2927 Virginia Beach Boulevard
Virginia Beach, VA 23452

Interpretive Education, Inc.
Mall Plaza, Suite 250
157 South Kalamazoo Mall
Kalamazoo, MI 49007

J & S Software
140 Reid Avenue
Port Washington, NY 11050

Jini Micro Systems, Inc.
P.O. Box 274
Riverdale, NY 10463

JMH Software of Minnesota
4850 Wellington Lane
Minneapolis, MN 55442

Kinetic Designs
401 Monument Road
Jacksonville, FL 32211

Krell Software Corporation
21 Millbrook Drive
Stony Brook, NY 11790

Lazer Micro Systems, Inc.
1791-G Capital
Corona, CA 91720

Math Software
1233 Blackthorn Place
Deerfield, IL 60015

Matrix Software, Inc.
325 Mario Avenue
Big Rapids, MI 49307

Med Systems Software
P.O. Box 2674
Chapel Hill, NC 27514

Merlan Scientific
247 Armstrong Avenue
Georgetown, Ontario Canada

Micro Gnome
5843 Montgomery Road
Elkridge, MD 21227

Micro Learningware
P.O. Box 2134
Mankato, MN 56001

Micro Software Systems
P.O. Box 1442
Woodbridge, VA 22193

Micro Technology Unlimited
2806 Hillsborough Street
Raleigh, NC 27605

Micro-Ed
P.O. Box 24156
Minneapolis, MN 55424

Microphys
2048 Ford Street
Brooklyn, NY 11229

Micro-Spec, Ltd.
2905 Ports O'Call Court
Plano, TX 75075

Minicomp Systems
5666 Stanley Street
Halifax, Nova Scotia B3K 2G1
Canada

Minnesota Educational Computer Consortium
2520 Broadway Drive
St. Paul, MN 55113

Mumford Micro Systems
Box 400
East Summerland, CA 93067

Plus Software
P.O. Box 1152
Angelton, TX 77515

Precision People, Inc.
P.O. Box 17403
Jacksonville, FL 32216

Professional Software, Inc.
166 Crescent Road
Needham, MA 02194

Program Design, Inc.
11 Idar Court
Greenwich, CT 06830

The Program Store
4200 Wisconsin Avenue
Northwest
Washington, DC 20016

Programs for Learning
P.O. Box 954
New Milford, CT 06776

PS Software House
P.O. Box 966
Mishawaka, IN 46544

Real Soft
1450 West Georgia Street
Vancouver, BC V6G 2T8
Canada

Right On Programs
P.O. Box 977
Huntington, NY 11743

Sensible Software, Inc.
6619 Perham Drive
West Bloomfield, MI 48003

Sirius Software, Inc.
2011 Arden Way, #2
Sacramento, CA 95825

Skyles Electric Works
231-E South Whisman Road
Mountain View, CA 94041

Snappware
3719 Mantell
Cincinnati, OH 45236

SOF-TEC
1043 First Avenue
Columbus, GA 31901

Softsel
8295 South La Cienega
  Boulevard
Ingelwood, CA 90301

Software Factory
515 Park Street
Anoka, MN 55303

Software Sorcery, Inc.
7927 Jones Branch Drive 400
McLean, VA 22102

Southeastern Software
6414 Derbyshire Drive
New Orleans, LA 70126

**Southing Swift Publishing
  Company**
1600 Fortview Road
Austin, TX 78704

Spectral Associates
141 Harvard Avenue
Tacoma, WA 98466

Sunburst Communications
Washington Avenue
Pleasantville, NY 10570

SYBEX
2344 Sixth Street
Berkeley, CA 94710

Synergistic Software
5221 120th Avenue Southeast
Bellevue, WA 98006

TYC Software
40 Stuyvesant Manor
Geneseo, NY 14454

United Software of America
750 Third Avenue
New York, NY 10017

Wesper Micro Systems
14321 New Myford Road
Tustin, CA 92680

3G Company
Rt. 3, Box 28A
Gaston, OR 97119

Appendix I

Taxonomy of Microcomputer Uses in Schools

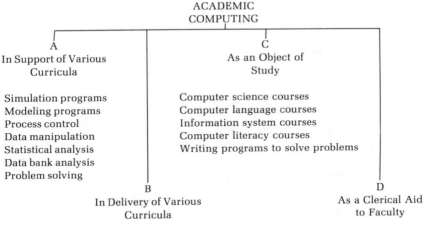

ACADEMIC
COMPUTING

A
In Support of Various
Curricula

Simulation programs
Modeling programs
Process control
Data manipulation
Statistical analysis
Data bank analysis
Problem solving

C
As an Object of
Study

Computer science courses
Computer language courses
Information system courses
Computer literacy courses
Writing programs to solve problems

B
In Delivery of Various
Curricula

Computer Aided Instruction
   — Drill and practice
   — Tutorial programs
   — Simulation
   — Gaming
   — Problem solving
Computer Managed Instruction
   — Organizing student data
   — Organizing curricula
   — Monitoring student progress
   — Diagnosing, prescribing
   — Evaluating learning outcomes
   — Planning for instructors
   — Remedial education

D
As a Clerical Aid
to Faculty

General test scoring
General test creation
Word processing

Microcomputers are used by teachers in the categories outlined here. The outline forms a taxonomy of computer uses in education in the United States. Explanations of each category follow. (See also page 73.)

A. National View of the Computer in Support of Various Curricula

In this category of computer use, students are required to execute problem solving tools used in the academic discipline at large. The discipline may be psychology, graphics design, history, math, or any other. The programs run interactively at microcomputers and they are sometimes attached to mainframes.

1. *Simulation Programs* emulate some aspect of the world: a chemical reaction, a lens design, a sun capturing a planet, an economy growing, a business failing, a population starving, etc.

2. *Modeling Programs* guide students in duplicating (mathematically) a process such as a social process, an engineering process, an energy process, a weather process, etc. Well known programs such as GPSS often receive the modeling information as data input.

3. *Process Control* uses the microcomputer to control some process such as the capturing of data from sensory probes; the repeated control of lights, cameras, or voltages in experiments; the control of drill presses, lathes, and other machines or the control of animals or humans through the duration of an experiment.

4. *Data Manipulation* programs are used in nearly all disciplines as a basic method for handling lists, statistics or numbers associated with an academic discipline. The computer can scan lists or files of data to sort them, select from them, compare them, or associate them analytically. Students may be assigned to write such programs, or may execute existing programs.

5. *Statistical Analysis* applies statistical procedures such as chi square or multiple regression to files of data. The data often result from surveys, or may come from lists of data supplied by authorities in the discipline. Several national data banks exist to which students connect their microcomputers by telephone.

6. *Data Bank Analysis* requires students to experience vari-

ous methods of analyzing large data files. Census files, economic data files, and political and social science files are often obtained from the University of Michigan, where 200 universities maintain 300 large files. The analysis often involves sorting or comparing, rather than statistical analysis.

7. *Problem Solving* programs are written by students as assignments in which they solve some problem in their discipline. Such problems often involve the execution of a standard formula which is too lengthy for manual calculation, such as the calculation of planetary orbits, mortgage payments, etc.

B. National View of the Computer in the Delivery of Various Curricula

1. *Computer Assisted Instruction* attempts to engage the student interactively in lesson materials related to the discipline. The student executes the programs, sometimes with no human teacher present, receiving drill and practice, tutorial materials, simulations, games, and problem solving experiences which carefully guide the student into new ideas and which require active responses from the student. CAI is sometimes used in twenty-minute modules of homework assignments, or sometimes in twenty to forty hours of continuous coursework. Human teachers may or may not be part of this process.

2. *Computer Managed Instruction* is used by teachers to assist the normal learning and tutoring process. Various files of information about student test results and about the curriculum can produce weekly diagnoses of where each student stands in the learning progression and can prescribe individualized remedial assignments to strengthen weaknesses. A file of test questions and answers is usually associated with such systems. These instructional management systems help instructors to organize the curricula and student data, monitor student progress, diagnose and prescribe, evaluate final outcomes, and plan for future curricular improvements.

3. *Remedial Education* applies game, simulation, and tutorial programs to children who test below grade level in the basic skills areas.

C. National View of the Computer As an Object of Study

1. *Computer Science Courses* provide students direct encounters with computer hardware and software. A variety of experience is appropriate, covering micro, mini, mainframe machines, and multiple languages. The principles which underlie various computer languages, operating systems, data base systems, file handling systems, and algorithm development are taught. Students often perform daily and weekly assignments which require considerable hours of computer use.

2. *Computer Language Courses* are offered to computer science majors and as a service to many other disciplines. Students experience the writing of application programs in languages such as FORTRAN, COBOL, APL, PL-1, Assembler, BASIC, PASCAL, and others. Considerable computer power is consumed by these users.

3. *Information System Courses* require students to use computer methods for classifying data, organizing information, keyword indexing, and structuring of data. This science underlies the work of librarians, archivists, scientists, and researchers.

4. *Computer Literacy Courses* provide elementary encounters with computer applications. Some universities require all students to take this course. By 1985, most entering freshmen will have received this experience in secondary schools, but adult learners will continue to benefit from these courses. Some literacy courses focus on the history of computing, others on the social impact, others on the future of computing, others survey the languages. All are justified.

5. *Writing Programs to Solve Problems* is at times assigned by teachers in all disciplines to focus attention on the computer as a tool within the discipline. In this experience, the student learns how to use a computer, write a program, execute it, modify it, and document it. These experiences are related to the curriculum (as in Section A) but underscore to the student the universality of the tool.

D. National View of the Computer As a Clerical Aid to Faculty

1. *General Test Scoring* enables teachers to use printed answer sheets with their multiple-choice tests. An optical scanning unit or a microcomputer then receives these answers, scores the test, and reports on the outcomes for each question. The reports and grades are then returned to the professor and students. In this form of computer use, no diagnosis or other services accompany the system, in contrast to the CMI (Computer Managed Instruction) systems. This test scoring facility is one aspect of larger comprehensive CMI systems and is often the first CMI module to be implemented.

2. *General Test Creation* is accomplished when all the biology instructors (for instance), state-wide in consortium or individually, pool all of their test questions. Held in a computer file, tests can then be constructed automatically by subject area, level of difficulty, and form of question. Unique tests can be generated for each student, the level of difficulty remaining nearly equal for the entire class.

3. *Word Processing* systems allow faculty (and students who pay a fee) to rapidly revise, edit, and publish textual materials. Departmental reports, articles for journals, class manuals, documentation of procedures, goals and objectives, financial statements, grant applications, research publications, and government grant reports are typical publication areas.

Index

Quality Education Data, 31

Radio Shack, 13, 32, 37, 41, 63, 116
Rent, renting, 15, 17, 18, 49, 117, 118
Resources, 4, 12
Robots, 81, 84
ROM level, 38
Royalties, 34, 36, 37, 40-42, 110

Sales ad, 60
Schools, 4, 7, 10, 18, 19, 50, 51, 54, 55, 57, 60, 63, 66, 71, 84, 95, 96, 97,
       105, 116, 118, 145-149
Schoolteachers, 3, 7, 84
Screens, 14, 33, 42, 71, 72, 74, 84, 90, 116, 118
Sell, selling, 5, 27, 28, 29, 40, 41, 59, 60, 63, 65, 70, 102, 108, 118
Seminars, 7, 23, 45, 47, 49, 50, 54, 56
Sensing devices, 84, 86
Set-up mode, 74
Small business, 3, 8, 29, 69, 70, 74, 90, 95, 101
Software, 5, 7, 8, 12, 20, 21, 25, 27-34, 36-42, 48, 52, 54, 71, 72, 77, 95,
       97-99, 101, 102, 108, 110, 116
   agents, 29, 34, 36, 38-40, 42, 119, 135
   authors, 29, 30, 34, 36, 38, 39, 41, 42, 118
   companies, 99, 101, 119, 140-144
   directories, 29, 119, 133, 134
   dispensers (see Software, vending machines)
   educational (see Educational software)
   expert, 101
   protection, 33, 40
   store, 93, 95, 101, 102
   theft, 33, 40
   vending machines, 101
Space vehicles, 81, 118
Speakers, 5, 14
Speech output devices, 84
Speeches, 56
Statistical systems (see Systems, statistical)